For Sharon you're well into
I know you'll find
bread but I hope you'll find
some exciting turnovers here.
Have a ball with this book.
Surely appreciate having
your mother's favorite orange
roll recipe which is a valuable
addition. We always look
forward to them when we are
guests at her home.
Sincerely
Dora Black

# Bread Baking Made Easy

# Bread Baking Made Easy

## Dora D. Flack

*Photography by Borge B. Andersen*

*Food stylist Janet Schaap*

Bookcraft

SALT LAKE CITY, UTAH

Library of Congress Catalog Card Number: 84-70368
ISBN 0-88494-524-3


First Printing, 1984


Lithographed in the United States of America
PUBLISHERS PRESS
Salt Lake City, Utah

*To the memory of*

*my mother*

*who taught me to bake bread*

## BREAD

*Be gentle when you touch bread.*
*Let it not lie uncared for and unwanted.*
*Too often bread is taken for granted.*
*There is so much beauty in bread:*
    *Beauty of sun and soil,*
    *Beauty of past toil.*
*Winds and rains have caressed it,*
*Christ often blessed it.*
*Be gentle when you touch bread.*

                      *Authorship unknown*

## THE THANK-YOU NOTE

*It was one of those days cast in gray,*
*Sky and heart and the feel of the day,*
*And nothing minted of earth or strange*
*And precious fabric could make it change*
*Until you sent me a loaf of bread*
*You made yourself. I saw your head*
*Over a blue bowl, over a book*
*Reading the recipe, love in your look,*
*Strength in your fingers, and your heart*
*Yielding the secret, golden part*
*That makes this more than fine spun wheat,*
*That makes the heart and the gray day sweet,*
*With the curious leaven one can blend*
*In a golden loaf of bread for a friend.*

Gladys McKee

# Contents

# Acknowledgments

For over thirty years I have been developing and innovating bread recipes. Most of them in this book are my own. However, many friends have shared their own favorite bread and roll recipes with me and they are given credit in the respective titles.

Other ideas for recipe development have often come to my attention in casual conversations, along with specific problems of people who are allergic to wheat and other grains; these ideas have resulted in new experiments. After all, there are a few basic ingredients in every bread. Beyond that, variety results from brainstorming and testing.

Considerable research in the field of grains has been necessary, especially as I have tried to assist friends with grain allergies, thus broadening the value of the book.

I would like to thank many individuals for their ideas, recipes, and constant encouragement as well as skilled assistance in proofreading the manuscript and galleys.

Neighbors, friends, and family have cheerfully sampled and approved, or disapproved and suggested, through all the testing processes. Some recipes I have tested as many as ten times to reach a point of perfection (I hope). No recipe in this book has been accepted without being tested, and in many cases adjusted, in my home lab-kitchen.

To the publishers and editors who have urged and suggested through long months of testing and writing I owe a debt of sincere gratitude, as well as to all of these people: Virginia Addams, Audrey Arthur, Eve Bean, Darlene Burrows, LaVerne Darrington, Lilian DeLong, Karla Erickson, Geraldine Felt, Myrtle Flack, Karen Hall, Mabel Miller, Olive Nielsen, Nola Paulsen, Dick Platt, Iva Price, Eve Rhodes, Nadine Riddle, Vernice Rosenvall, Lois Roylance, Della Scott, Marlane Smith, Helen Squire, Louise Squire, Vivian Talbot, Martha Tornblom, and Susan Weagel.

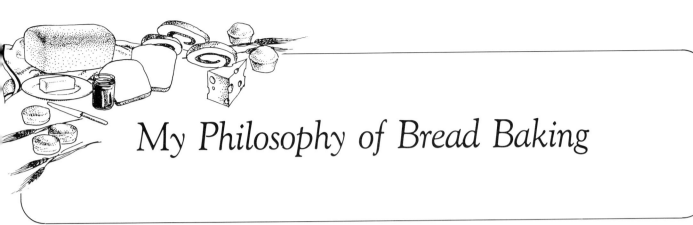

# My Philosophy of Bread Baking

Homemade bread—bread made with love—is far more than physical food. It satisfies the soul as well as the body. No fragrance in the world evokes such a multiplicity of emotions as does the smell of home-baked bread. The same odor may emanate from a bakery, but only when we walk into a *home* does the aroma affect us so forcefully, releasing a host of intangibles: feelings of nostalgia, memories, warmth, security, familiar sounds, contentment, nourishment, and a longing for the home baker, perhaps now gone.

For the home baker, nothing matches the inner satisfaction of providing the "staff of life" for those he or she loves. Why relegate that privilege to an impersonal commercial bakery where there is little concern for *your family* and where you do not know what goes into the loaves? *You care!*

My friend Martha says: "The aroma makes people open up to communication. In our home lived Eduardo, an exchange student from Germany, the son of a former Nazi officer. Eduardo seldom talked, yet I knew he had problems to unravel. As he came from school some days I had fresh bread just out of the oven; I would be ironing or sewing so that he would talk, thinking that I was absorbed otherwise. He often cleaned up half a loaf of fresh bread with a jar of jam. Communication barriers were tumbled and I could help him as he enjoyed the bread and talked. Without that aroma and fresh bread, he would have continued to keep everything bottled up inside.

"But the therapy works both ways," Martha continues. "Even though I'm now a working mother, at least once a week I *have* to get my hands into dough with yeast. It makes a woman feel as if she has truly created a home. My husband and children know this when they walk into that fragrance. Even if women have careers they are still domestic by nature, and bread making fulfills that need."

The very act of inhaling deeply on "Ummmm!" and exhaling on "Fresh bread!" invites relaxation, as children rush in from school. As a hungry child grabs a slice of bread from a commercial wrapper, he exhibits haste and impatience. On the other hand, it takes time to carefully cut warm bread, thus inviting sharing moments and a gracious atmosphere. We all *need* moments together to relax, savor, and communicate. Such opportunities must be created.

Homemade bread not only nourishes family members, but gives assistance, solace and love to others in need. For a sick neighbor a loaf of quality homemade bread invites healing—and confidences. "When you surprise me with a loaf of warm bread," one neighbor remarked, "it's far more than physical bread—it's friendship, and love too."

Such small gestures of friendship hark back to my own childhood when we little girls ran Mother's bread to neighbors' homes, lifting spirits as well as filling stomachs.

When I was only eight, my father died, leaving Mother with three little girls to support. Of course she went to work. At the young age of nine, I remember how tired my small hands became from kneading bread on my lunch hour while one of my sisters fed me a sandwich. We lived only half a block from school, so we always went home for lunch, and at least once a week bread had to be made. The bread "raised" all afternoon and was baked in the coal stove for dinner.

Counting pennies was our way of life. Mother didn't buy compressed yeast cakes. Instead (as she had learned at home) she kept a quart bottle with a "start" made from "everlasting yeast" which was fed daily with water drained from boiling potatoes; a pinch of sugar was added to feed the yeast. Not until many, many years later did I realize the bonus of that potato water.

When Mother remarried and was able to stay home, what a treat for us to return to a warm house, the aroma of fresh bread wafting out to gather us in. Homemade bread was an important budget stretcher.

Many years later, while I was serving a mission for the Church in Minnesota, one of the members in St. Paul frequently invited missionaries home after our midweek evening service. Enjoying her fresh bread and honey always generated a desperate longing for my distant home and family. That bread was a bridge to home.

After I was married and my husband, LeGrand, was in college, our tiny apartment had no oven. However, a week before our first baby was born, another blessing arrived in the form of an apartment-size electric range. Since then we have enjoyed homemade bread continuously. I can't even remember the last time I bought a loaf.

In 1951 I became a very young Relief Society president and the bishop challenged me to teach the women how to use our stored wheat. Vernice Rosenvall, Mabel Miller, and I put our heads and skill together for that purpose, which resulted in the first whole wheat cookbook, *Wheat for Man: Why and How*, which is still popular.

From section 89 of the Doctrine and Covenants we read: "In consequence of evils and designs which do and will exist in the hearts of conspiring men in the last days, I have warned you, and forewarn you, by giving unto you this word of wisdom by revelation. . . . *All grain is good for the food of man. . . .*" (D&C 89:4, 16; italics added.)

Recent research is supporting all phases of the 150-year-old Word of Wisdom, including the use of grains. I have enjoyed combining "all grains," knowing that one complements another; this produces better nutrition at low cost. I never worry about the "designs of conspiring men" because I know what goes into my bread when I bake it myself.

It is frequently said, "The way to a man's heart is through his stomach." True. Even career women and moms on the go can improve the family nutrition as well as creating that intangible "security blanket." Some recipes in this book are designated "Quick & Easy" for those whose schedules are especially tight so that cooks will know which ones best fit into tight timing. Remember also that even though bread takes a minimum of one to two hours from start to finish, not all that time is consumed in the bread-baking process. Other tasks are accomplished while one is waiting for rising and baking. With the aid of an electric bread mixer, marvelous bread can be made in a couple of hours. Suggested baking shortcuts and the combining of preparation processes reduce dishwashing.

Many recipes can be handled in phases, even when a woman must rush off to work in the morning and manage a three-ring circus at night. Bread can be mixed in the morning before she leaves for work, put in pans, covered with plastic, refrigerated, and then baked in the evening. Or conversely, it can be mixed at night and baked in the morning. Some recipes require constant surveillance and stirring down during rising, while others do not. Rushed working women will avoid the first kind.

Cooking experimentation has been and continues to be a way of life for me in my private laboratory, which is my own kitchen, of course. My tools and environment are like any other homemaker's. Problems of friends motivate me to pursue interesting experiments. For example, some people who suffer from celiac disease can't eat *any* wheat products, neither refined white flour nor whole wheat. Some can't tolerate any type of gluten, even the small amounts in grains other than wheat. These people can never enjoy a piece of toast or a sandwich. For celiacs I have developed a few successful recipes, as well as recipes for diabetics.

As a result of urging from many people, I have tried to bring together down-to-earth findings in this book. It is not a "health book" but includes white flour as well as whole wheat and other grains. I hope those who have an aversion to anything but white bread will be challenged to skip down the path of promise to more exciting baking experiences. Please don't be intimidated by lengthy instructions. The recipes herein are intended to instruct even the least experienced young cooks. I *want* you to succeed! Too many recipes leave questions in the minds of novice cooks.

My experiments have required much patience, which is not one of my innate qualities. I can still hear my mother quoting to me:

> If a string is in a knot,
> Patience will untie it.
> Patience will do many things;
> Did *you* ever try it?

Many of my bread problems have been like knots in string, requiring patience and persistence to unravel them.

Another axiom Mother often quoted was: "If at first you don't succeed, try, try again." That has also kept me moving in the face of apparent bread failures. I've learned from all of them.

Now, before you embark on your exciting bread-making adventures, one last bit of advice. One evening years ago, after enjoying a dish of Jim

Hunter's superb ice cream at the local ice cream parlor, I asked, "Jim, what's the secret of your ice cream?"

His eyes twinkled. "After I mix all the ingredients together, I add just a little bit of love."

That is the most important ingredient in bread —as in Jim's ice cream. I always add quite a bit of love. And it returns in beautiful nutritious bread. I use only the best ingredients for best results. Know your ingredients. Learn how to handle bread dough and treat it as a friend instead of a foe. Practice makes perfect! With practice you *will* learn how to control it. Although electric mixers are time savers and benefactors, they are not absolutely necessary to produce high-quality bread. I love to knead the dough. It's *alive!* Amazingly, frustrations can be worked out by kneading dough vigorously and even slamming it when you're upset. Good therapy.

Then, when I knead that beautiful bulk into loaves, they always receive an extra love tap. Your efforts are amply rewarded by appreciation from family members and friends who know you love them and care enough to satisfy hungers of the soul as well as of the stomach.

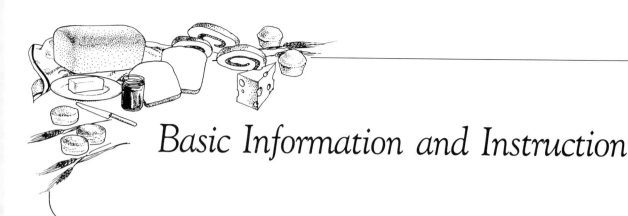

# Basic Information and Instruction

Long ago I remember reading a story in which a young man was having difficulty choosing a wife. He was on the verge of a decision but was still uncertain.

His mother's advice was: "Just happen by her house when you know she's making bread. Watch how she cleans the dough out of the mixing pan. If she leaves dough in the pan to be washed away, don't marry her. She'll be wasteful and will throw more out the window than you can bring in the door."

Bread baking is synonymous with frugality and becomes a lifelong practice—line upon line, precept upon precept.

Learning is like a sponge. When a little water is sprinkled over an absolutely dry sponge, the water often rolls off, or only a bit soaks in. A little more water, added without delay, finds soft spots on the sponge. As more water is added, the sponge absorbs and expands. From experience, I know that I can learn from almost anyone and I am constantly absorbing new techniques which I am eager to share. Therefore, even experienced cooks may find herein new facets to enhance their bread jewels.

Since everyone wants to succeed, I have made an earnest effort to write *elementary*, complete instructions. In this section a few imperative basics are explained briefly, with much more detail in the Ingredients and Equipment sections. Be sure to absorb it all for optimum success.

First of all, are you afraid to work with yeast? Take heart. All successful bread bakers can remember their beginning fears. You want to succeed, and I want you to succeed.

Through the years I've found that bread failures are rare; the successes far overshadow the occasional batch of bread that isn't up to standard. So don't despair if your first efforts fall short of expectation. Practice makes perfect.

Accurate measurements are important. So learn how to measure correctly.

*Flour and Dried Milk or Buttermilk:* Dip from canister with dry measuring cup. Level with spatula or flat-edged knife.

*Granulated Sugar:* Same as for flour.

*Powdered Sugar:* Spoon lightly into dry measuring cup. Level with spatula or flat-edged knife.

*Packaged Mix, or Quick Mix:* Spoon lightly into dry measuring cup over waxed paper. Level as above. Mix will be lumpy, of course. Pour excess from waxed paper back into box.

*Baking Powder, Baking Soda, Cream of Tartar, Salt, and Spices:* Dip into container and fill measuring spoon. Level as above.

*Grated Cheese, Shredded Coconut, Raisins, Chopped Nuts:* Pack lightly into dry measuring cup and level as above.

*Shortening:* Pack firmly into dry measuring cup. Level and remove with rubber scraper.

*Butter or Margarine:* Use wrapped sticks or cubes for easy measuring. Unwrap and cut with knife. Note printed measurements already on wrapper.

*Honey, Molasses, and Corn Syrup:* First, measure the shortening or oil for a recipe; then, after emptying the measuring cup, pour in the honey or molasses or corn syrup. Because of the greasy cup, the sweetening will slide out easily. Remove the residue with a rubber spatula. Follow this procedure except when the whole amount of honey or molasses must be added to the yeast before the oil.

*Milk and Other Liquids:* Set a liquid measuring cup on the counter, pour in the liquid, and bend down to check the correct amount at eye level.

Accidents are preventable, so obey the *Ten Commandments of Cooking Safety:*

1. Turn the saucepan handles on the range away from you to prevent their catching onto anything or tipping over.

2. After washing your hands, dry them to avoid slippery fingers and shocks from electrical outlets.

3. When chopping or paring foods, always turn

*Facing page:* Basic White Bread (p. 12); 100% Whole Wheat Bread (p. 22); bread in pans ready for oven

the sharp edge of a knife or vegetable parer away from you and your hand.

4. Avoid burns by using thick, dry potholders or heavy, padded mitts.

5. In mixing bread or other batters, you must sometimes scrape the sides of the bowl while the beaters are in operation. Keep the scraper right against the sides of the bowl so the scraper won't catch in the beater blades or the bread hook.

6. Turn off your mixer and unplug it whenever putting in or removing beaters.

7. Never disconnect an appliance by pulling the cord. Pull the plug instead.

8. Never allow small children on the counter when appliances are in operation. Hands and long hair can become easily entangled, resulting in serious injury.

9. Know your appliances and what they will and will not do. Read the manufacturer's instructions.

10. Wipe up spills immediately to avoid slippery or sticky floors.

## Cook's Preparations
(Especially for the beginner)

1. Does your schedule allow sufficient time to make a particular recipe?

2. Read the recipe completely to make sure all the ingredients are available and to know the time involved.

3. Tie back your hair if it's long. Wash your hands and wear an apron.

4. Assemble all ingredients and utensils on a tray to make sure you haven't forgotten anything.

5. Clean up as you proceed. Use one measuring cup for dry ingredients and one for liquids to eliminate extra dishwashing. The same is true of measuring spoons. As you finish using a utensil, put it in warm, soapy water to soak. Then dishwashing and cleanup is a breeze.

## Know Your Equipment

Good equipment is a must. *Please* refer to the Equipment section, after the recipe sections, for necessary utensils and tools. If you're on a tight budget, make these purchases from part of your food money because they are a long-term investment. By baking your own bread, in time you will save more than enough to compensate for purchasing proper equipment.

Especially note pan sizes as specified in recipes.

## Helpful Oven Hints

*Temperature:* Different ovens register slightly different temperatures. Know what your oven does and what adjustments you must make for success. Test it with an oven thermometer to determine where the dials should be set for accurate temperatures. An oven thermometer is inexpensive. Two oven temperatures and baking times are given in the recipes herein because of oven variances and altitude.

*Rack Positioning:* You can easily change the positioning of oven racks to accommodate various baking needs. *Cookies* should be baked on the top position, *cakes* on the middle position, and *pies* on the bottom position. *Bread* is usually baked on the middle position, or on the lowest for a crustier bottom. You might try baking *rolls* on the top position because they are made from smaller bits of dough, but this will also depend on your pans and your oven.

*Proper Browning of Products:* Sometimes rolls brown too much around the edges of a cookie sheet and not enough in the middle. Dark tin absorbs instead of reflects and may not conduct heat evenly. A cookie sheet with sides restricts air circulation. Aluminum cookie sheets without sides will spread heat evenly for browning biscuits and rolls. However, use them only when rolls are not to be crowded together. Some recipes instruct you to place rolls quite close together so they rise upward rather than spreading out.

(To ascertain if a baking pan or sheet is aluminum, test with a magnet. The magnet will not cling to aluminum.)

Uneven browning may occur if you are using two cookie sheets in the oven at one time. You will obtain better results by using only one sheet at a time. Check to see if the cookie sheet is too big to permit the circulation of hot air in the oven.

Because glass absorbs heat faster than metal, lower the baking temperature by 25° F. when using glass baking dishes.

If your bread is overbaked on top and not browned on the bottom, it is probably because the rack should be moved down to the bottom position, or because the bread pans are too shiny. Shiny, new bread pans do not promote browning on the bottoms of loaves. To speed the darkening process of bread pans, temper them by placing them in the oven and turning the dial to 400° F. Leave the pans in for an hour and turn off the oven. Leave the pans in while they are cooling. Restaurant supply houses sometimes have heavy-duty pans which are already dull. Hardware stores and supermarkets usually carry inexpensive bread pans. Avoid pans lined with white; they do not brown properly.

*Facing page:* Yam or Sweet Potato Bread (p. 21); Eve's Vegetable Bread, and vegetable dough in bowl (p. 30); Yam Buns (p. 22); Della's Sesame Braids (p. 27)

Be sure to check the equipment section of this book before purchasing equipment. Buy the correct sizes.

*Air Circulation:* Do not overcrowd the oven. Circulation is imperative. Allow at least an inch between pans when several loaves are baking at once. For perfect loaves, place the pans only on one rack at a time, even if you must re-knead part of the loaves to wait for the first ovenful to bake. Allowing circulation space minimizes "cracking" of the crust.

## Know Your Ingredients

For the beginner, here are a few basic ingredient facts. However, consult the Ingredients section for more detail and for required ingredients which may be unknown to you. I have made suggestions for availability.

### Liquids

"Warm," "lukewarm," or "hot" are all relative terms. This is why you need a thermometer. A candy thermometer is fine. "Lukewarm" water would be "cool" to the touch of most people. "Warm" water is what most people might call hot tap water. The temperature of 115° F. is just right for the yeast; consistently in the recipes this is termed "warm water." Any reference to "hot water" will mean water heated on the burner, but not to the boiling point.

Be sure to read the Ingredients section to learn about other useful liquids.

### Yeast

Your first fear with yeast breads is that you'll not treat the yeast correctly for optimum results. Many books refer to dissolving yeast as "proofing." This simply means that the yeast is being activated as it dissolves in the liquid. A pinch or teaspoon of sweetening, added with the yeast, speeds activation.

On your first attempt, when adding the yeast and sweetening to the warm water, take time to watch the yeast in the cup or small bowl. In 3 to 5 minutes you'll see little spurts of tan explode under the water and rise to the top. This tells you the yeast is "activating" or "dissolving." When the top of the water has patches of tan, or is covered with a smooth tan appearance from these little explosions, the yeast is ready to use.

There are two ways to treat the yeast-dissolving process:

1. You can dissolve the yeast in a small bowl or cup and add a little sweetening; when the yeast is dissolved, add the liquid to other ingredients in the large mixing bowl.

2. Pour the warm liquid into the big mixing bowl, then add the yeast and sweetening. Let stand a few minutes. When the yeast is dissolved and is activating, add the other ingredients in that same bowl. This method saves dishwashing.

Read more about yeast and using yeast in the Ingredients section.

Salt and fat tend to slow yeast action. Therefore, both are usually added with the other ingredients *after* yeast is activated or dissolved.

### Flour

The very nature of wheat makes it impossible to give undisputed flour measurements. Because flour varies so much, two amounts are generally given in these recipes—for example, "3 to 4 cups all-purpose flour." This means that you never add more than the minimum amount (3 cups) while kneading until you determine that a little more is actually necessary to form a good elastic ball of dough. Seldom should you add more than the maximum amount (4 cups) and only if really necessary to keep it from sticking while working with it.

Humidity makes a difference in the necessary amount of flour. Some wheat has a higher moisture content; therefore, the flour also retains more moisture.

The protein content of wheat and flour also makes a difference in the bread. If buying wheat from which to grind your own flour, try to get at least 12 percent protein, and higher if possible. A higher protein count makes better bread.

### Making a Sponge

Check the Equipment section for different kinds of beaters. Good bread can be made without an electric mixer, but a heavy-duty slotted spoon is essential for beating bread ingredients. I find that the slotted spoon works better than a wooden spoon. But you need a wooden spoon also, especially for sourdough recipes.

Usually a "sponge" is made first with all the ingredients and only the first measurement of flour. A sponge is about the consistency of cake batter. Usually the sponge rests about ten to fifteen minutes to begin the rising or fermentation process, after which the remaining flour is added gradually to make the dough. As the sponge batter becomes thick enough to start climbing electric beaters, finish the stirring in the same bowl with either a slotted spoon or a wooden spoon. During the sponge "resting time," accomplish a short task elsewhere in the house, but set the timer to call you back to the bread in process.

## Kneading

Don't be afraid of kneading. You can *learn* to knead—and enjoy it. After beating the sponge and adding more flour, you have worked up a mass of unmanageable dough. Turn it out onto a floured surface. At first the mass seems hopelessly sticky. Gather the dough with your fingers, working in the flour until you can handle it with your whole hand. Now knead with the *heels* of your *hands* to get a good kneading action, working in additional flour *only as necessary* to keep it from sticking to the breadboard. Keep the dough as soft and pliable as possible for lighter, more tender bread. As you knead, the dough becomes more pliable and easier to handle until you have a wonderfully alive ball with tiny bubbles forming on its surface.

The terms "sticky dough," "soft dough," and "stiff dough" need a little explanation. Sticky dough is like a batter—too thick to stir easily but not stiff enough to handle with hands. Soft dough is pliable, spongy, and elastic, and does not hold its shape very well. It spreads. Stiff dough means that the ball has become hard to knead and lacks good "spring."

If you get the dough too stiff, try adding one-fourth cup warm water, even after it has been kneaded. Poke your fingers into the dough. Fill the little holes with water, then knead it all over again until it is well mixed. This is messy, but it is better than leaving it too stiff. "Soft" dough, of the proper consistency, will stick to your fingers a bit even at the end of the kneading process. This is as it should be.

You'll unconsciously find a rhythm to the kneading. Remember, you are working with a live product which responds to your touch. With practice, it becomes fun. Kneading eight to ten minutes produces excellent bread.

Use a spatula to clean all the dough residue from the mixing bowl. Or, as stated before, dust with a bit of flour and it comes out easily with your hand. Most recipes elsewhere instruct you to grease a clean bowl and turn the ball upside down so that the greased surface is on top to prevent it from drying out. To cut down on dishwashing, however, I simply put the dough back in the almost-clean bowl with the smooth side up. It's beautiful! Then I cover it securely with plastic wrap so the dough doesn't dry out.

## Rising

Let the dough rise in the bowl for about an hour, unless the recipe specifies differently. Room temperature makes a difference in rising time. If the room is cool, rising is slower. You may want to place the bowl in the oven, turning on the dial for a couple of minutes until the temperature reaches about 85° F. to 90° F., but no warmer. Turn off the dial and keep the oven door shut while your dough is rising. Or put the bowl in warm water in the sink. If dough rises too fast in too warm a place, fermentation is disturbed, resulting in coarse-textured bread with an off-flavor. It is important to avoid this if you want high-quality bread.

## Forming Loaves and Rising in Pans

When the dough has risen in the bowl to about double in bulk, it is ready for the pans. To test it, poke two fingers into the risen dough; if it is ready, the prints will remain. Turn out the dough onto a lightly floured surface.

A rubber scraper works wonders in removing all the dough from the mixing bowl and from your hands and fingers—or try dusting the dough with a bit of flour and rubbing it off.

In shaping loaves, I knead them, but that comes from years of practice. You may have better success by rolling each loaf portion into a flat oblong about a foot long. Fold over one-third and press out the air bubbles, then fold the other one-third over the first fold, again forming an oblong. Press well, to eliminate holes or air bubbles, then roll as for a jelly roll from the short side. Some people deftly mold a loaf in their hands, up off the table. Experiment until you find the best method for *you*.

When using regular bread pans, I place the loaves to one side in the pan for better rising. Make the loaf rectangular or oblong rather than humped in the middle. Do not fill the pans more than half or two-thirds full.

For whole wheat bread, as soon as the loaves are shaped and placed in the pans, put each pan with the dough in it into a plastic bag, fold over the opening, and clip it shut with a spring clothespin or paper clip. This prevents drying out, improves texture, and speeds rising. When the loaves have risen once, remove them from the bags, punch down and remold the loaves, and place them again in the bags. When the loaves have doubled in bulk a second time, remove them from the bags. If you like, for a little different appearance (like buttercrust bread), slash the tops down the middle with a sharp knife. This also prevents cracking on the sides during baking.

I use bags only for whole wheat bread. For other bread I simply cover the loaves with a piece of plastic wrap to prevent their drying out.

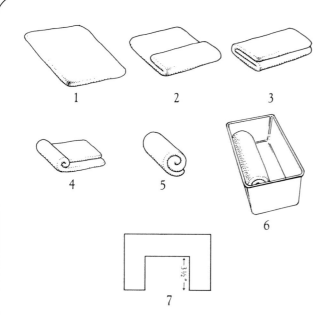

If bread rises too high in the pan, the result is coarse-textured bread. *Never put it in the oven at this stage.* Take the time to punch down and remold each loaf. I get so involved sometimes that I re-knead more than twice before baking (once it was four times)—and I discovered that the bread was even better textured. It had stretching cracks on the sides, but the bread was superb and very elastic.

Devise a "rising gauge" in order to know the right height for bread to reach in the pan. Take a thin piece of cardboard. Cut out an opening in the bottom center wide enough to fit over your bread pans and 3½ inches high for white bread or 3¼ inches high for whole wheat. Then, when you think the loaves are about high enough for baking, set this gauge over the loaves on the counter and you will see if they actually are high enough. Don't, however, let them rise any higher than the opening. If they do, punch down and remold the loaves. Save this gauge to use each time you bake. You'll find it most helpful.

Try variety in forming loaves. Form your dough like French bread into long oblong shapes or large round balls and bake them on greased cookie sheets. Again, this is not for beginners. If you want a crustier bread, grease the back of a cookie sheet and let the bread rise and bake there. A heavier crust is formed because the airflow is not inhibited.

For quality bread in a good size for the toaster or sandwich bag, do not use the large, squatty pans. Buy pans (see Equipment section) no larger than 9" x 4½". This makes a big difference in the bread, especially with whole wheat.

## Baking

Usually we *pre*heat the oven for baking bread, which takes about ten minutes with an electric range. I have found that in most cases, I can avoid that preheating time if I put the bread into a cold oven and then turn the dials. Sometimes (not always) I must add another five minutes onto the total baking time, testing with my knuckles for doneness. (If the bread is done, it sounds hollow.) I wouldn't recommend this for a beginner, who should use a preheated oven.

For a very crusty bread, you may wish to purchase a clay "stone" and paddle at a specialty shop. Or refer to page 56 for information on the use of unglazed quarry tiles for this purpose. This is not for beginners, however. A brick in a shallow pan of water on the bottom of the oven also improves crustiness, as does brushing the loaves with water with a pastry brush or spraying them with water every five to ten minutes during baking time. Keep a separate spray bottle for such purposes.

## Phase Baking for Tight Schedules

Even people who are away from home most of the time can enjoy the marvelous aroma and thrill of fresh-baked bread by making the bread in phases, or stages, although the bread isn't as near perfection. Mix the bread at night and bake in the morning, or vice versa. Actually this "fermentation," or rising time, is too long, but not impossible.

Mix the bread (say at night) and form into loaves. Place in greased bread pans. Grease the tops, too. Place the pans of dough in plastic bags. Refrigerate immediately. Rising will continue over the seven to ten hours of refrigeration, whichever fits your working schedule. The lesser time is preferable. Next morning as soon as you're up, remove the pans from the refrigerator. Take the pans out of the bags and place in the cold oven. Turn dials to the proper temperature. Add five minutes to baking time. Fresh bread for breakfast! The top may blister; in this case, lower the baking temperature 25 degrees next time, or lower the baking rack in the oven. This bread is usually not quite as light as bread made under ideal conditions.

Tap the bread with your knuckles when the timer rings. If the loaf sounds hollow, it's done; otherwise, return it to the oven for five minutes.

## Cooling

When the bread is done, use thick pot holders to lift the pans from the oven. You may wish to leave the loaves in the pans for five or ten minutes to set the cells, but this is not imperative. Turn them out onto a wire rack to cool. Do not leave them tipped upside down; set them on racks *topside* up for better shape. If you prefer a soft, tender crust, brush the tops with a little butter while the loaves are still hot and cover them with a towel. For a crisp crust, do not grease the loaf; allow it to cool uncovered. The cold loaves should be stored in plastic. In hot weather, store them in the refrigerator, or freeze them.

## Slicing

Now your bread is done and ready for slicing. If you simply can't wait for it to cool, go ahead and enjoy it hot. However, be sure to use a serrated bread knife to cut it. A good knife is essential. Heat the blade on a stove burner for a few minutes first. The hot knife slices the hot bread beautifully without collapsing the loaf. It works better for me to lay the loaf on its side and saw gently without applying pressure. You can learn to cut bread so it looks as professional as baker's bread.

Please read the whole book so you can better learn how to proceed intelligently and avoid disaster.

Have you read all basic instructions?

*"Homemade bread is the yeast of home."*
George Magnusson

# Basic White Bread with Ten Variations

(For an explanation of any unfamiliar ingredients listed in these recipes, see
the discussion on Ingredients in the last section of this book.)

Since most people use all-purpose flour, we'll begin bread baking with a Basic White Bread recipe. Do not use self-rising flour for bread because it already contains some leavening agents. At the end of this first recipe you will find many variations for your convenience and adventure. Bread making should never become monotonous. Many variations to this one recipe prove that it can be a never-ending challenge.

## Basic White Bread

(See photograph on page 5)

*Yield: 2 loaves, 1½ pounds each (double the recipe for 4 loaves)*

2 ½ cups water (115° F.) (potato water if available)
1 tbsp active dry yeast
¼ cup honey or sugar
3 cups all-purpose flour
1 tbsp salt
¼ cup margarine (half a cube)
3 to 4 cups more all-purpose flour

1. Pour water into small mixing bowl.
2. Sprinkle in yeast and add sweetening. Let yeast dissolve, without stirring. Yeast will form a tan coating over water in 5 or 10 minutes. Don't let it stand so long it becomes light and foamy and loses its life.
3. While yeast is dissolving, sift together 3 cups flour and salt into large mixing bowl. Add margarine to flour and with pastry blender cut in margarine to resemble crumbs.
4. Add yeast mixture to flour crumbs. With slotted spoon, beat well to make a sponge. Cover with plastic wrap and let stand 10 to 15 minutes.

5. Gradually add more flour to the sponge, never exceeding the lower measurement of 3 cups, adding only enough flour to make a soft dough.
6. Turn out onto well-floured surface and knead 8 to 10 minutes, adding flour only as necessary to prevent sticking.
7. Return dough to bowl and cover with plastic. Let rise about an hour or until double in bulk.
8. Punch down and divide dough into 2 portions.
9. Shape into loaves and put in greased loaf pans (8 ½" x 4 ½"). Let rise.
10. For superior texture, punch down and remold loaves for a second rise in pans.
11. When dough is almost double in bulk, bake 30 to 35 minutes at 375° F. to 400° F., or until done. (Rap top of loaf with knuckles and it will sound hollow.)
12. Remove from pans and cool on wire racks.

**Tip:** Save water from boiled potatoes and refrigerate for bread making. Heat it to 115° F. If necessary, use part plain water and part potato water.

## Half-and-Half Whole Wheat Bread

*Yield: 2 loaves*

Use Basic White Bread recipe but substitute whole wheat flour for first 3 cups of the all-purpose flour. Using whole wheat flour first allows the bran in the whole wheat to soak a bit. At the last, kneading is easier with white flour than with whole wheat flour. Proceed with other ingredients and instructions as given in recipe. The finished bread may not be quite as light as white bread, but so good! Bake at same time and temperature.

# Potato Bread

*Yield: 2 loaves*

Use Basic White Bread recipe. Heat water to 120° F. With wire whip, beat in 6 tbsp potato flakes. Potato water can also be used, if available. *Or,* use about ½ cup leftover mashed potatoes and plain water. This makes bread more tender. Proceed with rest of ingredients and instructions as given. Bake at same time and temperature.

# Whole Millet Bread

*Yield: 2 loaves*

Use Basic White Bread recipe. Cook ½ cup millet seeds in 1 cup water for 10 to 15 minutes and cool. Liquid is almost completely absorbed. Add cooled millet to the yeast-liquid mixture when flour is added. Proceed with rest of ingredients and instructions as given. Bake at same time and temperature.

Millet offers protein enrichment and a chewier texture.

# Ground Millet Bread

*Yield: 2 loaves*

Use Basic White Bread recipe. Grind ⅓ cup dry millet seeds in blender and use with first addition of flour. Proceed with rest of ingredients and instructions as given. Bake at same time and temperature.

# Buttermilk White Bread

*Yield: 2 loaves*

Use Basic White Bread recipe. Substitute buttermilk for water, same amount. In small saucepan heat buttermilk to 115° F. In the same saucepan, add yeast and sweetening and let yeast dissolve, then proceed with rest of ingredients and instructions. *Or,* dried buttermilk (follow measurements on can) can be sifted with flour; use plain warm water for prescribed amount of liquid.

# Sugarless Bread

*Yield: 2 loaves*

Use Basic White Bread recipe, leaving out sweetening and adding 1 tbsp dimalt (see Ingredients section) to yeast and water. Caution: Use water no hotter than 110° F. and no cooler than 90° F. when using dimalt. Add yeast-dimalt mixture to flour and shortening, beating well with slotted spoon, then proceed with remaining instructions. Let rise once in bowl, twice in pans. Bake at 375° F. to 400° F. 35 to 40 minutes. Pans can be placed in a cold oven as it is turned on. Dimalt produces a crustier bread of excellent texture. Excellent for diabetics and hypoglycemics.

# Hot Dog and Hamburger Buns

*Yield: 6 to 8 buns (from one-loaf portion of a preceding recipe)*

Make your own hot dog or hamburger buns from the Basic White Bread recipe or any of its variations.

For hamburger buns, roll the reserved portion of dough with the rolling pin to about 5/8 inch thick. (With my utensils I keep two sizes of empty tin cans, one for large buns and one for small.) Punch out the buns as you would punch rolled cookie forms. Place the rounds of dough on a greased cookie sheet. Cover with plastic wrap and let rise until double in bulk. Bake at 375° F. to 400° F. for about 20 minutes or until golden brown.

For hot dog buns, cut the loaf portion of dough into strips (about 8 per loaf portion). Roll dough pieces with palms of hands on the kneading surface until you have fat oblong strips. Let rise double in bulk on a greased cookie sheet and bake like hamburger buns.

These can be frozen for future use.

You'll never buy another hamburger or hot dog bun.

# Cheese Bread

*Yield: 2 loaves*

From Basic White Bread recipe, reserve one portion of dough. Grate ½ to ¾ cup cheddar cheese. Roll dough into rectangle and sprinkle with cheese, pressing it into dough. Roll tightly as for jelly roll. Bake 35 to 40 minutes at 375° F. to 400° F.

# Raisin Bread

*Yield: 2 loaves*

Use Basic White Bread recipe. I reserve one portion of the dough and mix in ⅓ cup sugar, 2 tsp cinnamon, and 1 cup raisins, plumped in hot water in a bowl. Instead of re-molding this loaf a second time in the pan, let it rise while the other loaves rise twice and it will be ready to bake at the same time. This bread makes superb toast.

# "Convenience" Frozen Bread

*Yield: 3 smaller loaves*

Use the Potato Bread recipe above, but double the amount of yeast.
1. Let bread rise once after it is kneaded. Grease 3 loaf pans (about 7 ½ ″ x 3 ½ ″).
2. Divide dough into three portions (about 1 pound 2 ounces each).
3. Shape loaves and place in greased pans. Brush tops with oil. Cover with plastic wrap and freeze solid (about 2 hours).
4. *Or*, make two loaves and use the third portion for dinner rolls. For dinner rolls, roll dough into a thick rectangle. With a pizza cutter cut off bits 2 inches square. A one-third portion of the recipe makes 16 rolls. Roll into balls. Place on greased cookie sheet, oil tops, cover with plastic, and freeze solid (about 2 hours).
5. As soon as loaves and balls are frozen solid, remove from pans. You may have to pour hot water over bottom of pans to dislodge the loaves. Balls will lift off easily.

6. Return to plastic bags and keep frozen until ready to use.
7. For dinner rolls: Remove balls as needed. They can be baked on a greased cookie sheet or in a greased standard muffin tin, or a dozen may be baked together in an 8-inch square cake pan.
8. Brush generously with butter or oil and let thaw and rise at room temperature to desired size (1 to 2 hours). Or, see quick-rising method following step 12. Dough will not rise during baking time.
9. Bake 25 to 30 minutes at 350° F. to 375° F. Serve piping hot.
10. For loaves: Remove loaves as needed for baking. Place loaves in greased loaf pans (same size as above). Cover with a towel and let thaw and rise at room temperature until dough is about 1 ½ inches above top of pan (takes about 3 to 6 hours, depending on room temperature).
11. Bake at 350° F. to 375° F. for 30 to 35 minutes, or test for doneness with knuckles.
12. Remove from oven. Turn out onto wire rack to cool. Brush with butter or shortening.

## QUICK-RISING METHOD:

Place frozen bread dough in greased pans. Place a pan with ½ cup water on bottom of oven. Preheat oven to 150° F. and place bread dough in oven, *turning dial to Off position*. Don't let oven get too hot. Cover loaves with towel and let rise almost 3 hours. *Remove towel* and turn oven dial to 375° F. to 400° F. Bake 35 to 40 minutes or until done. Remove from oven. Turn out onto wire rack to cool and brush with butter or shortening.

N ow that you have the basics in mind about white bread and you've tried the Basic White Bread recipe with marvelous success, let's consider whole wheat, which is somewhat different. Be sure to check the Ingredients section to learn about whole wheat flours.

The whole wheat kernel is a marvel of God's creations, and I firmly believe we can't improve on the balance of nutrients in that kernel. I have long been a devotee of whole wheat cooking and would encourage others in the effort. Nothing exceeds the full flavor of whole wheat in cooking, unless it's mixing other grains with it, thus multiplying nutritive values.

The Half-and-Half Whole Wheat Bread recipe calls for mixing whole wheat flour with the white. Once you've done that, you may be daring enough to use all whole wheat flour. There are other whole wheat bread recipes later in the book.

The secret of making good whole wheat bread is keeping the dough soft, just stiff enough to handle. The stiffer the dough, the drier and heavier the bread will be.

Check the Ingredients section about dough conditioner and gluten flour, which are pluses for whole wheat bread.

Once you're into whole wheat, you will enjoy *Wheat for Man: Why and How*, a complete recipe book using whole wheat. You'll be stretching your food budget by baking your own bread. And baking with whole wheat flour saves even more when grinding your own flour from the whole kernel. With a little determination and practice, you'll discover that it fits into your time budget as well as your food budget. With an electric bread-mixer I can make excellent whole wheat bread in 2 to 2 ½ hours from start to finish.

One last bit of advice: *If at first you don't succeed, try, try again.*

*"There is no royal road to anything. One thing at a time, all things in succession. That which grows fast, withers as rapidly; that which grows slowly endures."*

Anonymous

# Yeast Breads

(For an explanation of any unfamiliar ingredients listed in these recipes, see
the discussion on Ingredients in the last section of this book.)

*QUICK & EASY*

## One-Bowl Raw Potato Bread

**(Takes 2 hours or less)**

*Yield: 2 loaves*

2 medium-sized potatoes (about 2 cups)
2 cups warm water (120° F.)
2 tbsps active dry yeast
2 tbsps sugar
¼ tsp ginger
⅓ cup dried milk
1 tbsp salt
6 to 6 ½ cups all-purpose flour (half white and half
   whole wheat flour can be used)
⅓ cup wheat germ
¼ cup vegetable oil

1. Peel and finely grate potatoes into large mixing bowl. Or potatoes can be peeled and chunked, then pureed in the blender with the 2 cups of hot water.
2. Pour hot water over potatoes. This will cool the water.
3. Lightly stir in yeast, sugar, and ginger; let yeast dissolve.
4. Sift together dried milk, salt, and 2½ cups of the flour.
5. Add wheat germ, oil, and sifted dry ingredients to mixture in mixer bowl. Beat 2 to 3 minutes on medium speed or beat vigorously with slotted spoon.
6. With spoon stir in about 2 cups more flour to form a soft dough.
7. Turn out onto generously floured surface.

Knead in as much flour as necessary to make a soft ball.
8. Place dough back in bowl. Cover with plastic wrap and let rise until double in bulk (about 30 to 45 minutes).
9. Punch down and divide into two portions.
10. Form loaves and place in greased 8½″ x 4½″ pans. (This recipe makes 2 high-rise loaves. You may wish to make 3 loaves instead. Let them rise no more than double. If using half whole wheat flour, form only 2 loaves.)
11. Let rise until double and bake 30 to 35 minutes at 350° F. to 375° F., or until done.
12. Turn out and cool on wire rack.

*QUICK & EASY*

## Raw Potato Dinner Rolls

*Yield: Using the One-Bowl Raw Potato Bread recipe, make one loaf of bread. Take the other portion and make two dozen rolls.*

### METHOD #1
1. Pinch off small portions a little less than golf-ball size and form balls.
2. Roll tops in greased muffin cups, then turn top side up.
3. Or whip a small egg with a wire whip and brush tops of dough.
4. Let rise half an hour or a little less and bake 20 to 30 minutes at 375° F. to 400° F.
5. Serve hot or cool.

## METHOD #2

1. Roll out dough on floured surface into a rectangle almost ½ inch thick.
2. With pizza cutter, cut into 2 dozen diamond shapes.
3. Place on greased *back* of cookie sheet.
4. Brush with beaten egg and sprinkle sesame or poppy seeds on top.
5. Let rise almost half an hour and bake as above. This makes an excellent hard roll.
6. Remove carefully with spatula. Serve hot or cool.

# Buttermilk Bread (White)

*Yield: 2 loaves*

### Cook's Corner

*If you have not discovered the wonder of buttermilk, don't delay longer. The browning is a little darker but beautiful and even. The texture is excellent, the flavor is superb, and buttermilk is easy on the digestive tract.*

2 cups buttermilk
1 tbsp active dry yeast
3 tbsps honey
¼ cup butter
3 cups all-purpose flour
2 tsps salt
½ tsp baking soda (optional)
2 to 3 cups more all-purpose flour

1. In medium-sized saucepan, heat buttermilk to 115° F. and add yeast and honey.
2. As soon as the yeast starts to dissolve, add butter to soften.
3. Measure and sift together 3 times the 3 cups flour, salt, and soda.
4. Pour yeast mixture into large mixer bowl and add sifted dry ingredients. Beat 3 minutes on medium speed.
5. With wooden spoon, stir in 2 cups more sifted flour and mix well.
6. Turn dough out onto floured board and knead 8 to 10 minutes.

7. Return dough to bowl. Cover with plastic wrap and let rise in warm place about 1 hour.
8. Punch down and divide into 2 equal parts. On lightly floured surface, form 2 loaves.
9. Place loaves in greased loaf pans (8½" x 4½"). Cover tops with plastic wrap and let rise until double in bulk.
10. Punch down. Remold loaves. Let rise again.
11. Bake 30 to 35 minutes at 375° F. to 400° F. or until done.
12. Turn out on wire rack to cool.

Double the recipe for 4 loaves.

**Tip:** Dried buttermilk can be used in place of fresh. Sift ½ cup buttermilk powder with flour and use 2 cups warm water (115° F.) to soften the butter; then proceed according to the rest of the instructions.

**Tip:** Adding ½ tsp baking soda speeds rising somewhat but is not absolutely necessary.

## VARIATION:

Dimalt is successful in this recipe. But be sure the liquid is no hotter than 110° F. Substitute 1 tbsp dimalt for the full amount of honey.

*"The man who deals in sunshine is the man who wins the crowds. He does a lot more business than the man who peddles clouds."*

Anonymous

# Half-and-Half Buttermilk Bread

*Yield: 2 loaves*

2 cups buttermilk (115° F.)
2 tbsps active dry yeast
¼ cup honey
2 eggs, well beaten
¼ cup oil
½ cup mashed potato, or potato flakes
2 ½ cups whole wheat flour
1 tbsp salt
¼ tsp soda
2 to 3 cups all-purpose flour

1.  In medium-sized saucepan, heat buttermilk. Remove from heat.
2.  Sprinkle yeast over buttermilk and add honey. Let yeast dissolve.
3.  In large mixer bowl, beat eggs.
4.  Add oil, mashed potato, and yeast mixture.
5.  Sift together whole wheat flour, salt, and soda. Add to ingredients in mixer bowl. Beat 3 or 4 minutes.
6.  Let rest 10 minutes.
7.  With slotted or wooden spoon, stir in up to 2 cups more flour gradually. When dough is stiff enough to knead, turn out onto floured board and knead 8 to 10 minutes until a good elastic ball is formed.
8.  Let rest while greasing 2 loaf pans.
9.  Divide dough into 2 equal portions. Form loaves.
10. Place in greased 8½″ x 4½″ pans. Let rise in plastic bags or cover with plastic wrap.
11. When dough is doubled in bulk, turn loaves out and remold.
12. Let rise again in pans until almost double in bulk.
13. Bake 30 to 35 minutes at 350° F. to 375° F. or until brown. (Buttermilk causes darker browning and you may wish to lower temperature 25°.)
14. Remove and let cool on wire racks.

**Tip:** Dried buttermilk can be used. Sift ½ cup dried buttermilk powder with whole wheat flour, salt, and soda. Substitute 2 cups of water for the 2 cups of liquid buttermilk.

## VARIATION:

Dimalt is successful in this recipe. Be sure liquid is no hotter than 110° F. Substitute 1 tbsp dimalt for the full amount of honey.

# 100% Whole Wheat Buttermilk Bread

*Yield: 2 loaves*

### Cook's Corner

*Use electric bread mixer for best results with this recipe.*

2 cups buttermilk (115° F.)
2 tbsps yeast
2 tbsps honey
2 eggs
¼ cup oil
¼ cup leftover mashed potato or flakes
2 tsps salt
¼ cup gluten flour
5 to 5 ½ cups whole wheat flour

1.  In medium-sized saucepan, heat buttermilk. Sprinkle in yeast. Add sweetening and let yeast dissolve.
2.  In large mixer bowl, beat eggs well. Add oil and mashed potato. (Change beater to dough hook if using electric bread mixer.)
3.  Sift together twice the salt, gluten flour, and 3 cups whole wheat flour.
4.  Add yeast mixture to mixer bowl.
5.  Add sifted dry ingredients gradually, beating 4 or 5 minutes on medium speed, scraping sides.
6.  Let rest 5 to 10 minutes.
7.  If using bread mixer, add remaining flour gradually until it begins to clean sides of bowl. Beat 4 to 5 minutes longer. If kneading by

hand, change from beaters and stir in rest of flour with a slotted or wooden spoon.

8. Turn dough out onto oiled surface. Knead to a good ball.

9. Divide into two portions and mold into two loaves. Place in greased loaf pans (8½″ x 4½″). Cover with plastic wrap and let rise until double in bulk.

10. Punch down and remold loaves. Cover for a second rise in pans.

11. Bake 30 to 35 minutes at 375° F. to 400° F.

**Tip:** Dried buttermilk can be used. Sift ½ cup dried buttermilk powder with whole wheat flour, salt and soda. Substitute 2 cups of water for the 2 cups of liquid buttermilk.

**Tip:** Dimalt does not work well in this recipe for me.

# Cereal Bread

*Yield: 2 loaves*

½ cup warm water
2 tbsps active dry yeast
½ cup molasses or honey
¾ cup water, boiling
¾ cup oatmeal, preferably quick-cooking
1 cup buttermilk
⅓ cup vegetable oil
2 cups all-purpose flour
1 tbsp salt
½ tsp soda
3 to 3½ cups all-purpose flour

1. In a small bowl, put yeast in water with part of molasses. Let yeast dissolve.

2. Boil ¾ cup water in medium-sized saucepan and stir in oatmeal. Cook 2 or 3 minutes. If using old-fashioned oats, cook a few minutes longer.

3. Remove from burner and add buttermilk, oil, and remaining molasses, which will cool the cereal.

4. Sift together 2 cups flour, salt, and soda and add with yeast mixture to ingredients in saucepan. Beat with slotted spoon.

5. Let rest a few minutes.

6. Add all-purpose flour gradually. When stiff enough for kneading, turn dough out onto floured surface and knead 8 to 10 minutes until soft, elastic ball forms.

7. Place dough in bowl and let rise, covered with plastic wrap, until double in bulk, about 1½ hours.

8. Punch down dough and divide into 2 portions.

9. Let rest 10 minutes, then form into loaves.

10. Place loaves in greased pans 8½″ x 4½″. Let rise until double in bulk.

11. Bake 45 to 50 minutes at 350° F. to 375° F.

12. Remove from oven and turn out to cool on wire rack.

**Tip:** If using dried buttermilk, use 1 cup water and add ¼ cup dried buttermilk powder to other sifted dry ingredients.

## VARIATIONS:

1. Any leftover cooked cereal can be substituted for cooked oatmeal; this measurement can be adjusted a little according to the amount of your leftover cereal. Use cooked cracked wheat, cooked cornmeal, Cream of Wheat, or whatever you have.

2. Use ¾ cup 100% Bran cereal, soaked in ¾ cup of hot water as a substitute for other cooked cereal and proceed according to the rest of the instructions.

3. You can make this recipe with sweet milk instead of buttermilk, using the same amount and eliminating the soda.

4. Substitute 1 cup whole wheat flour for one cup of the all-purpose flour.

*"Homemade bread is lovin' from the oven."*

# Dick's Diabetic Bread

*Yield: 4 loaves*

## Cook's Corner

*This recipe was developed to be made in an electric bread mixer. Although you can make it by hand kneading, it will not be as fine-textured.*

2 cups raisins
4 cups pure apple juice, unsweetened
4 tbsps active dry yeast
½ cup vegetable oil
2 tbsps salt
6 cups whole wheat flour
4 eggs, well beaten
7 to 8 cups all-purpose flour
3 tbsps cinnamon
1 cup sunflower seeds

1. Place raisins in bowl of hot tap water and let stand a few minutes to plump them.
2. In medium-sized saucepan, heat apple juice to 115° F. Pour into large bread mixer bowl.
3. Add yeast to apple juice and let stand a few minutes to dissolve.
4. Beat eggs and add with yeast to juice in bread mixer bowl. Add oil, whole wheat flour, and salt.
5. Beat thoroughly 4 to 5 minutes to develop gluten. Let rest a few minutes.
6. Add all-purpose flour gradually, then cinnamon; beat a few minutes longer.
7. Add sunflower seeds and raisins. Beat to distribute them throughout the dough.
8. Let rest a few minutes while greasing 4 loaf pans 8½" x 4½".
9. Turn dough out onto oiled kneading surface and cut into 4 portions. Form 4 loaves and place in pans.
10. Cover with plastic wrap and let rise until double in bulk in pans.
11. Punch down. Turn out and remold loaves.
12. Let rise a second time in pans until almost double in bulk.
13. Bake 35 to 40 minutes at 375° F. to 400° F. or until it tests done.
14. Remove from oven and turn out onto wire rack to cool.

## VARIATION:

For 100 percent whole wheat bread, add 500 mg. vitamin C crushed between 2 spoons or 1 tbsp dough conditioner with the yeast. Substitute 1 cup gluten flour for one cup whole wheat flour and use enough flour to make dough stiff enough to begin pulling from sides of bread mixer bowl. All other instructions are the same.

*QUICK & EASY*
# Oatmeal Molasses Bread

*Yield: 2 loaves*

½ cup boiling water
1 cup quick-cooking oatmeal
2 tbsps active dry yeast
1 cup warm water (115° F.)
⅓ cup vegetable oil
½ cup molasses
½ cup canned milk
2 tsps salt
2 eggs, beaten
6 cups sifted flour
1 tsp anise flavoring (optional)
1 cup dates or raisins (optional)
1 cup chopped nuts or sunflower seeds (optional)
¼ cup wheat germ (optional)

1. In a small saucepan, boil ½ cup water.
2. Add yeast to 1 cup warm water in large mixer bowl.
3. Add oatmeal to boiling water in saucepan.
4. Add oil, molasses, salt, and canned milk to oatmeal.
5. Beat eggs well.
6. When yeast is dissolved in mixer bowl, add oatmeal mixture and eggs.
7. Add 3 cups flour gradually and beat well, then add more flour gradually to make a soft dough, mixing the last part with a wooden spoon.
8. Turn out onto floured surface and knead well.
9. Add optional ingredients as desired and knead well to distribute them thoroughly.
10. Place in bowl. Cover and let rise until double in bulk.

11. Divide into 2 portions and form 2 loaves.
12. Place loaves in greased pans 8½" x 4½" and let rise until almost double in bulk. Bake 35 to 45 minutes at 350° F. to 375° F.
13. Remove from oven and cool on wire rack.

**Tip:** This bread can be mixed and allowed to rise once in bowl for about ½ hour. Form into two loaves. Cover with plastic wrap, refrigerate immediately, and leave for 7 to 9 hours, whichever is convenient with your time schedule. Remove from refrigerator and let stand at room temperature while preheating oven. Bake as above. The texture will be a little coarser but the bread is still delicious.

# Yam or Sweet Potato Bread

(See photograph on page 6)

*Yield: 3 loaves*

### Cook's Corner

*At our home we love yams. Since the jumbo size are so much cheaper, that's what I buy. This often means leftovers. Since regular potatoes are an excellent addition to bread, why not yams? I began experimenting and discovered that yams not only make a delicately flavored bread, but the color is just as delicate. This bread always makes a hit when served to guests. It also makes exceptional toast.*

1 cup leftover yam (baked or boiled or candied) (If yams are candied, cut sugar and oil to 1 tbsp each in making bread.)
1 cup buttermilk
1 tbsp active dry yeast
2 tbsps sugar
2 tbsps butter
1 egg
¼ tsp soda
2 tsps salt
1 tsp nutmeg (optional)
4 to 6 cups all-purpose flour (the wide variance in the amount of flour depends upon how much water you use to blend the yams)

1. In a medium-sized saucepan, heat buttermilk to 115° F. Remove from heat.

2. Add yeast and sugar to buttermilk in saucepan and let yeast dissolve.
3. Blend yam, adding ¼ cup or a little more water, but only as necessary to mix it to the consistency of canned pumpkin. If you boiled the yams just for this recipe, use the cooking water.
4. Sift together 3½ cups of the flour, soda, and salt.
5. Beat egg in small mixing bowl.
6. In large mixer bowl combine egg, yam, buttermilk-yeast mixture, butter, and only part of sifted dry ingredients. This softens butter and it beats in well. Beat 3 minutes on medium to high speed.
7. Add remaining flour mixture gradually until dough starts to climb the beaters. With wooden or slotted spoon stir in enough more flour to reach kneading consistency.
8. Turn dough out onto floured surface and knead 5 to 8 minutes, adding flour only as necessary (no more than 6 cups) until a smooth elastic ball is formed.
9. Return dough to mixer bowl and cover with plastic wrap. Let rise in a warm place until doubled in bulk.
10. Punch down and return dough to bowl; let rise again until doubled in bulk.
11. Turn out onto floured surface. Divide in thirds and form 3 loaves.
12. Place in greased 7½" x 3½" pans. Let rise until almost doubled in bulk.
13. Bake 35 to 40 minutes at 375° F. to 400° F.
14. Remove from oven and turn out onto wire rack to cool.

## VARIATIONS:

1. 1 tbsp dimalt is good in this recipe substituted for sugar. Be careful that liquid is no hotter than 110° F.

2. Replace 2½ cups all-purpose flour with the same amount of whole wheat flour, mixing the whole wheat flour in as the first flour to be added.

# Yam Buns

(See photograph on page 6)

*Yield: 18 to 20 buns*

Use Yam Bread recipe.
1. After dough rises twice, pinch off golf-ball size bits and place in greased muffin tins.
2. Cover with plastic wrap and let rise until doubled in bulk, about 1 hour.
3. Bake at 375° F. to 400° F. 15 to 20 minutes.

If using 2 muffin tins with a dozen cups each, add water to empty cups to prevent burning tins.

## VARIATION:

One cup raisins or ½ cup sunflower seeds, or both, can be added.

*QUICK & EASY*
# Flat Bread

*Yield: At least 1 dozen pieces (can be cut in large or small portions)*

## Cook's Corner

*Here is an unusual hot bread for company, ready to serve in a little over an hour.*

2 cups water (115° F.)
1 tbsp sugar
1 tbsp active dry yeast
4 cups flour
2 tsps salt
½ cup margarine, melted
seasonings of your choice: sesame seeds, Parmesan cheese, herbs, onion, Lemon 'n Herb

1. In large mixing bowl, set yeast to dissolve in water with sugar.
2. Sift together flour and salt.
3. When yeast is activated, add sifted flour and salt and beat well.
4. Let rise about a half hour.
5. Grease jelly roll pan (11″ x 15″) and spread dough out flat in pan with heel of hand.

6. Melt margarine and pour over dough.
7. Sprinkle with seasonings and let rise until double in bulk (about half hour).
8. Bake 20 to 25 minutes at 400° F. to 425° F.
9. For serving, cut into squares with pizza cutter and serve piping hot. It's already buttered.

For a small number, cut recipe in half and bake in 8″ x 8″ square pan.

# 100% Whole Wheat Bread

**(Takes 2 to 2 ½ hours from start to finish)**

(See photograph on page 5)

*Yield: 4 loaves*

## Cook's Corner

*This bread is best made in an electric bread mixer, but it can be done by hand.*

5 cups warm water (115° F.)
1 tbsp dough conditioner, or 500 mg. vitamin C crushed between 2 spoons
2 tbsps active dry yeast (3 tbsps hastens rising)
⅓ cup honey
⅓ cup vegetable oil
2 tbsps liquid lecithin, or 2 eggs
⅓ cup potato flakes or powder, or about 1 cup left-over mashed potatoes
½ cup gluten flour
6 cups whole wheat flour
2 tbsps salt
4 to 5 cups more whole wheat flour

1. Pour water into large bowl of bread mixer.
2. Sprinkle in dough conditioner or crushed vitamin C, then yeast. Add honey and let yeast dissolve.
3. Sift together gluten flour, 6 cups whole wheat flour, and salt.
4. Turn bread mixer to low speed and add oil, lecithin, and potato flakes to yeast mixture. Stir, then add sifted dry ingredients and mix two or three minutes on medium speed to make a sponge. Let rest about 10 minutes.

5. Add remaining flour gradually, as needed, to make a soft dough which begins to clean sides of mixer bowl. On high speed mix 5 to 8 minutes, depending on your mixer.

6. Turn dough out onto surface which has been lightly oiled with about 1 tbsp of oil. Also oil your hands. This prevents sticking and makes handling whole wheat bread dough much easier.

7. Divide dough into 4 equal portions and let rest while greasing loaf pans 8½″ x 4½″.

8. Form loaves and place in greased pans.

9. Place pans of dough inside plastic bags.

10. Let rise in warm spot until double.

11. Remove from bags and remold each loaf.

12. Place pans in bags again and let dough rise until almost double a second time.

13. Remove from bags. Slash top of each loaf with a sharp knife or razor blade and bake in pre-heated oven 30 to 35 minutes at 375° F. to 400° F.

14. Remove from oven. Turn out onto wire racks to cool.

**Tip:** This dough can be placed in pans, covered with plastic, and refrigerated 8 to 10 hours. Put in cold oven. Set dials for 350° F. to 375° F. and bake 40 to 45 minutes or until done.

## VARIATIONS:

1. For sugarless bread use 2 tbsps dimalt with yeast and no sweetening. Water must not be more than 110° F. Sprinkle in dimalt with yeast, then proceed as usual. Caution: Do not refrigerate the dimalt bread and delay the baking.

2. For additional fiber and nutrition, cook 1 cup brown rice in 2 cups water. Simmer until all water is absorbed and the grains are fluffy. Add this to the bread with all the other ingredients. What a marvelous flavor and texture results! Bake as usual. The loaves are big and plump; high rises, I call them. The bread is soft and tender and stays fresh longer.

As you bring it out of the oven, pick off the hard-baked kernels on top which might pose a hazard to sensitive teeth.

Once you have tried this addition, it may become a good habit.

# Complete Protein Bread

*Yield: 4 loaves*

### Cook's Corner

*The amino acid lysine is weak in whole wheat. Split peas are rich in lysine. Therefore, by using a balance of split peas and whole wheat you can achieve a complete vegetable protein. I have worked out this recipe based on USDA papers covering the subject. A piece of cheese eaten with the bread complements the vegetable protein with animal protein, adding further enrichment.*

¾ cup golden split peas
1 ½ cups water
5 cups warm water (115° F.)
3 tbsps active dry yeast
⅓ cup honey
1 tbsp dough conditioner
2 cups oatmeal
½ tsp fennel or caraway seed
3 eggs, well beaten
⅓ cup vegetable oil
1 ½ tbsps salt
¾ cup gluten flour
½ cup potato flakes or powder, or ½ cup leftover mashed potatoes
5 cups whole wheat flour
6 to 7 cups more whole wheat flour

1. Soak ¾ cup golden split peas in 1 ½ cups water overnight or about 8 hours.

2. Into large mixer bowl, pour all the warm water. Sprinkle in yeast, dough conditioner, and honey. Let stand 5 to 10 minutes while yeast dissolves.

3. In a blender, grind oatmeal and fennel seed. Pour into dissolving yeast mixture but don't stir.

4. In blender, puree soaked split peas, adding ¼ cup more water only if needed. Pour into yeast mixture.

5. In small mixer bowl, beat eggs and add to yeast mixture.

6. Add oil, salt, gluten flour, potato, and 5 cups whole wheat flour. Beat on medium to high speed 3 or 4 minutes.

*Facing page:* Mother's Parker House Rolls (p. 38); Eve's Knot Buns (p. 41); Buttermilk Butterhorns (p. 42)

7. Let rest 10 to 15 minutes.

8. With beaters running on low speed, add more flour until dough begins to climb beaters. Turn off mixer. Clean off beaters and stir in remaining flour (up to six cups) with slotted or wooden spoon until it forms a soft dough. Do not add the last cup unless it is actually needed. In the bowl, mix by hand to form a ball of sorts. (If using an electric bread mixer, add flour until dough begins to pull from sides of bowl. Then turn to high speed and beat for 5 to 10 minutes, depending on your bread mixer's instructions. Then turn out onto oiled kneading surface.)

9. Oil the kneading surface and hands with about 1 tbsp vegetable oil. Turn out dough onto kneading surface and knead 8 to 10 minutes to a good elastic ball, adding a little more oil as necessary to prevent sticking.

10. Let dough rest while greasing loaf tins 8½″ x 4½″.

11. Cut into 4 equal portions and form loaves. Place in greased pans. Place dough in pan in plastic bags. Clip closed with a spring clothespin or paper clip and let rise until double in bulk.

12. Remove pans from bags. Turn out each loaf and remold, replacing loaves in the pans and then in the bags.

13. Let rise until almost double in bulk (use the rising gauge).

14. Preheat oven. Remove loaves from bags and bake 30 to 40 minutes at 375° F. to 400° F. or until bread tests done.

15. Remove from pans and cool on wire racks.

**Tip:** If you have a wheat mill, grind the split peas into flour and add to batter along with gluten flour.

**Tip:** For variety, mold one of the loaves into a ball and place on a greased cookie sheet. When it is ready for the oven, slash the top two or three times with a sharp knife or a razor blade, and slip it into the oven. Bake the same as the loaves and rap with knuckles for doneness.

## VARIATIONS:

1. Substitute 2 tbsps dimalt (see page 89) for the honey and be sure water is no more than 110°

F. As the wheat sprouts, it becomes a rich source of lysine. Therefore, this recipe not only becomes a highly nutritious sugarless bread, but its protein value is further enriched.

2. Add 2 cups cooked brown rice and bake bread in 5 loaves instead of 4. This adds fiber and tenderness.

QUICK & EASY
# Wheat Germ Buttermilk Bread

*Yield: 2 loaves*

2 cups buttermilk
2 tbsps active dry yeast
⅓ cup sugar
2 tbsps butter or margarine
1 egg
2 tsps salt
2 cups whole wheat flour
1 cup wheat germ
2 ½ to 3 cups all-purpose flour

1. In medium-sized saucepan, warm buttermilk to 115° F.

2. Remove from heat and add yeast and sugar.

3. When yeast is dissolved, add butter to mixture in saucepan.

4. In large mixer bowl, beat egg and add yeast mixture, beating thoroughly.

5. Add salt and whole wheat flour. Beat several minutes on medium to high speed.

6. With a slotted spoon, stir in wheat germ and part of the all-purpose flour, beating well.

7. Turn out onto floured surface and knead 8 to 10 minutes, adding flour only as necessary to prevent sticking badly.

8. Cover ball of dough on kneading surface with the large mixer bowl and let rest about 15 minutes.

9. Divide into two portions and knead into loaves.

10. Place in greased pans 8½″ x 4½″ and refrigerate at least 2 hours. Or leave it overnight in refrigerator.

11. Leave at room temperature while preheating oven. Bake 40 to 50 minutes at 350° F. to 375° F. Remove from pans and cool on wire rack.

**Tip:** This recipe is superb for making your own hamburger and hot dog buns. See Hot Dog and Hamburger Buns recipe in the Basic White Bread section for instructions on forming the buns. This recipe makes 2 dozen 6-inch hot dog buns and about 20 hamburger buns.

# Della's Sesame Braids

(See photograph on page 6)

*Yield: 3 loaves*

1 ½ cups milk
1 cup warm water (115° F.)
2 tbsps active dry yeast
¼ cup sugar
3 eggs
1 tbsp salt
¼ cup vegetable oil
approximately 7 ½ cups all-purpose flour
1 egg, for brushing tops of loaves
¼ cup sesame seeds

1. In a small saucepan, heat milk to 115° F.
2. In large mixer bowl, sprinkle yeast over water and add sugar. Let yeast dissolve.
3. Beat eggs *well*. Add eggs, oil, salt, and half of the flour and beat about 3 minutes on medium to high speed.
4. With a slotted or wooden spoon, beat in 3 more cups of flour gradually. When mixture is stiff enough to make a very soft dough, turn out onto well-floured kneading surface, preferably a pastry cloth, and knead until smooth and "blistered."
5. Return dough to the bowl, cover with plastic wrap or a damp towel, and let rise until double in bulk (about an hour).
6. Punch down and let rise again.
7. Cut dough into three portions. Then cut each portion into 3 more. Work one loaf at a time. Roll each small portion into "ropes" about 15 inches long. Roll and stretch with the palms of the hands.

8. Secure three ropes at the top by squeezing together, then braid loosely.
9. Place in greased loaf pans (8 ½ " x 4 ½ "). Let rise in pans until double in bulk.
10. With wire whip, beat the egg; brush tops of loaves with it. Sprinkle sesame seeds on top.
11. Bake 30 to 35 minutes at 375° F. to 400° F.

# Rye Bread

(See photograph on page 23)

*Yield: 3 loaves*

2 cups warm water (115° F.)
2 tbsps active dry yeast
¼ cup brown sugar
¼ cup molasses
¼ cup vegetable oil
2 tsps caraway seeds
½ tsp liquid anise flavoring
1 tsp vanilla
¼ cup instant mashed potato flakes or ½ cup leftover mashed potatoes.
2 cups rye flour
2 tsps salt
2 to 2 ½ cups all-purpose flour

1. Pour water into large mixer bowl. Add brown sugar and yeast. Let yeast dissolve.
2. Add molasses, oil, seeds, flavorings, mashed potatoes, 1 cup all-purpose flour, rye flour, and salt. Beat on high speed 2 to 3 minutes.
3. Let rest 10 minutes.
4. Clean off beaters and with a slotted or wooden spoon stir in remaining flour gradually, only enough to make a soft dough.
5. Turn dough out onto floured kneading surface. Knead about 8 to 10 minutes until it forms a soft, pliable ball.
6. Return the ball to the mixing bowl. Cover tightly with plastic wrap and set in a warm place to rise, about an hour, until double in bulk. Do not hurry it.
7. Divide into 3 equal portions. Form into long narrow loaves or round balls. For long loaves, roll each portion into an oblong, then roll as a jelly roll.

8. Rye bread, in my opinion, should be crusty. Using the backs of cookie sheets permits better air circulation in the oven. Grease the backs of 2 cookie sheets or 1 large one, which will accommodate three loaves at once, placed crosswise. Cover and let rise until double in bulk. If your cookie sheet will accommodate only two rolls, place the third on another cookie sheet and bake the single one first. Re-mold the other two loaves and let them rise a second time while the first is baking. A finer texture results from this second rise.

9. Slash loaves diagonally across the top three times before putting in the oven, if desired. For crunchier crust, spray the loaves with water as you place them in the oven and 2 or 3 times during baking. A shallow pan of hot water with a brick in it set on the bottom of the oven also adds to crust formation.

10. Bake 35 to 45 minutes at 350° F. to 375° F.

11. Remove from oven when done (sounds hollow when rapped with knuckles). Let stand a few minutes before removing with a spatula to wire racks to cool.

**Tip:** Lilian DeLong's rising cradles and unglazed tiles (see pages 55-56) are great for baking rye bread.

**Tip:** Rye dough is a little stickier than regular wheat dough.

## VARIATION:

This recipe makes 18 to 20 excellent rye buns. Roll out about 5/8″ thick. Grease or flour the edge of a drinking glass or a can and cut rounds. Place on greased cookie sheets and let rise, leaving space between for spreading and rising. Bake 15 to 20 minutes at 375° F. to 400° F. Serve hot or cold.

# Buttermilk Rye Bread

*Yield: 3 loaves*

Use Rye Bread recipe but add ½ cup dried buttermilk, sifted with first cup of all-purpose flour, or heat and substitute 2 cups of buttermilk for the water.

# Multiple-Grain Bread

*Yield: 2 big 2-pound or 3 smaller loaves*

### Cook's Corner

*Use alternative grains and seeds as desired or available. If all the grains listed below are not available, use what you have. The advantage of combining is that food value is enhanced. Where one grain may be weak in some elements, it is complemented by another. If gluten flour is not available, use 3 cups all-purpose flour in place of that much whole wheat flour.*

*Dimalt substituted for honey does not work well in this recipe.*

¼ cup oatmeal
2 tbsps barley
2 tbsps buckwheat
2 tbsps millet
2 tbsps brown rice, or ¼ cup rice flour
¼ cup cornmeal
¼ cup rye flour
¼ cup triticale flour
1 cup gluten flour
1 cup whole wheat flour
1 tbsp salt
3 cups warm water (115°F.)
2 tbsps yeast
1 tbsp dough conditioner or 500 mg. Vitamin C
⅓ cup honey
½ cup potato flakes, or about 1 cup leftover mashed potatoes
⅓ cup vegetable oil
2 tbsps liquid lecithin, or 2 eggs
1 tsp anise flavoring (optional)
2 tsps caraway seeds (optional)
2 tbsps sesame seeds (optional)
½ cup sunflower seeds (optional)
3 to 4 cups more whole wheat flour (this amount may vary, depending upon how many of the grains are used)

1. In blender on highest speed grind together, as fine as possible, the oatmeal, barley, buckwheat, millet, and rice.

2. Sift together cornmeal, rye flour, triticale flour, gluten flour, 1 cup whole wheat flour, and salt. Combine with grains from blender.

3. Into large mixer bowl, pour 3 cups warm water. Sprinkle in yeast and dough conditioner. Add honey. Let yeast dissolve.

4. Add potato, oil, lecithin or eggs, flavoring, and optional ingredients, then sifted dry ingredients; beat well, about 3 minutes on medium to high speed. Let rest 10 minutes.

5. With a slotted or wooden spoon, stir in 3 more cups of whole wheat flour, gradually, until stiff enough for kneading.

6. Oil the kneading surface and your hands with about 1 tbsp oil. Turn out dough onto oiled surface and knead 8 to 10 minutes. If using an electric bread mixer, beat 5 to 8 minutes. Then turn out onto oiled surface to form loaves.

7. Form loaves (2 big or 3 small) and place in greased pans (8½" x 4½" for both sizes). Let rise, covered with plastic wrap, until double in bulk.

8. Turn out loaves and remold. Let rise again.

9. If dough rises too fast and "gets away from you," knead a third time, then watch carefully. You won't ruin it by this third rise. If you have formed two loaves, let it rise to 3½ inches on the cardboard rising gauge. If you made three loaves, let them rise barely to the top of the pans.

10. Place in unheated oven. Turn dials to 350° F. to 375° F. Bake 40 to 45 minutes. Bread is done when it sounds hollow at the rap of your knuckles.

11. Turn loaves out to cool on wire rack.

"In the drama of existence—should you take a searching look, you will find the leading lady often is the cook."
Anonymous

# Pumpernickel Bread

(See photograph on page 23)

*Yield: 2 or 3 loaves*

2 ½ cups water (115° F.) (potato water if possible)
2 tbsps active dry yeast
⅓ cup molasses
1 tsp caraway seeds
¼ cup carob powder or cocoa
2 tbsps vegetable oil
1 cup mashed potatoes
2 cups whole wheat flour
2 tsps salt
½ cup cornmeal
3 cups rye flour
1 to 2 cups all-purpose flour

1. In large mixer bowl, sprinkle yeast over water, adding molasses. Let yeast dissolve.

2. Add caraway seeds, carob, oil, potatoes, whole wheat flour, salt, cornmeal, and rye flour. Beat until it begins to climb the beaters.

3. With a slotted or wooden spoon, stir in all-purpose flour gradually until dough is stiff enough to be turned out onto a floured kneading surface. Knead 8 to 10 minutes, adding flour only as necessary to keep it from sticking too badly, until it forms a rather stiff ball.

4. Return dough to the bowl. Cover with plastic wrap. To start and hasten the rising, set the bowl in a pan of warm water in the sink. Let dough rise until double in bulk, about 1 hour.

5. Turn out onto lightly floured kneading surface. Knead 5 minutes and return to bowl for a second rise until double.

6. Divide into 2 or 3 equal portions. Bake this bread in 2 regular loaf pans 8½" x 4½", or divide into 3 equal portions and form oval or round loaves which can be baked on the greased backs of cookie sheets or in round casserole dishes. For exceptional texture, remold loaves after they have doubled in bulk. Then let them rise a second time in pans before being baked. Cover during rising so they will not dry out.

7. Bake 1 to 1¼ hours at 350° F. to 375° F. Longer baking creates crustier bread. To form even heavier crust, spray with water 3 or 4 times during baking. Or place a shallow pan of hot water with a brick in it in the bottom of the oven.

8. Remove from oven, leave in baking pans 10 minutes, then turn out onto wire racks for cooling.

**Tip:** Here is another recipe that can be made into long loaves by the use of Lilian DeLong's "rising cradles" and unglazed quarry tiles (see pages 55-56).

# Iva's Variety Wheat Bread

**(For the bread mixer)**

*Yield: 3 high loaves*

3 ½ cups buttermilk
2 tbsps yeast
raw grated carrots, up to 1 cup
raw bran, up to 1 cup (not the bran cereal, but bran
   purchased at the health food store)
1 tsp baking soda
3 cups whole wheat flour
½ cup vegetable oil
½ cup sweetening of your choice
1 tbsp salt
3 eggs
4 to 5 cups whole wheat flour

1. In a medium-sized saucepan, heat buttermilk to 115° F. Remove from heat.
2. Add yeast and let it dissolve.
3. Grate carrots finely and combine with bran, baking soda, and 3 cups flour in buttermilk-yeast mixture. Beat and let stand about 10 minutes.
4. In the large bread mixer bowl place oil, sweetening, salt, and eggs.
5. Pour mixture from saucepan into bread mixer bowl. Add flour gradually until dough pulls away from the sides of the bowl. Mix 10 minutes.

6. Let dough rise in the bowl a half hour.
7. Punch down and form into 3 loaves. Place in greased pans 8 ½" x 4 ½". Let rise until double in bulk, about 30 to 40 minutes. Use the rising gauge to make sure dough does not rise too high.
8. Preheat oven to 400° F. As soon as bread is put into the oven, turn heat down to 350° F. Bake about 35 to 40 minutes or until done.
9. Remove from oven and turn out onto wire rack to cool.

## VARIATION:

Use other grains as desired as substitutes for bran and carrots, such as cooked buckwheat, oatmeal, millet, rice, or whatever you might happen to have on hand.

# Eve's Vegetable Bread

(See photograph on page 6)

*Yield: 4 high-rise or 5 not-so-high loaves*

### Cook's Corner

*Don't pass up this wonderful recipe. Here is a flavor and color you'll truly enjoy.*

½ cup finely chopped red cabbage
½ cup finely chopped onions
¾ cup grated carrots
⅓ cup finely chopped celery
¼ cup finely chopped green pepper
¼ cup finely chopped cucumber
¼ cup alfalfa sprouts
4 cups milk
2 tbsps active dry yeast
4 tbsps sugar
4 tbsps shortening
4 tsps salt
3 eggs, beaten
11 to 12 cups all-purpose flour

1. Prepare vegetables and set aside.
2. In large saucepan, scald milk. Add shortening to melt and cool to 115° F.
3. Add sugar and yeast. Let yeast dissolve.

4. In large mixer bowl, beat eggs. Add salt. Then add 5 cups of flour with vegetables and beat with a slotted spoon. Beat well and let rest 10 minutes.
5. Add 5 cups more flour gradually, beating with slotted spoon.
6. Turn out onto floured surface and knead 8 to 10 minutes.
7. Cover with plastic wrap and let rise until doubled in bulk.
8. Punch down and mold into loaves. Place in either 4 or 5 pans 8½" x 4½". Let rise until double in bulk.
9. Bake at 375° F. to 400° F. 35 to 40 minutes or until it tests done.
10. Remove from oven. Let stand 5 minutes in pans and turn out onto wire racks to cool.

**Tip:** If you don't have all the vegetables listed, use whatever you have.

QUICK & EASY
# Granola Bread

*Yield: 3 loaves, 1¼ pounds each*

1 ½ cups water (potato water is best)
1 cup yogurt or buttermilk
2 tbsps active dry yeast
½ cup honey
2 eggs
1 cup granola
1 tbsp salt
¼ cup vegetable oil
2 cups whole wheat flour
½ to 1 cup sunflower seeds
4 ½ to 5 cups all-purpose flour

1. In medium saucepan, heat water and yogurt to 115° F. Remove from heat.
2. Add yeast and honey and let yeast dissolve.
3. Into a large mixer bowl place eggs, granola, and salt.
4. Add yeast mixture, oil, and whole wheat flour and beat well.
5. Add 2 cups all-purpose flour and beat on medium speed at least 3 minutes.

6. With slotted spoon, gradually stir in sunflower seeds and 2 cups more all-purpose flour until dough is stiff enough to turn out onto floured surface. Add flour only as necessary to prevent sticking while kneading dough about 8 to 10 minutes until a soft ball is formed.
7. Divide dough into 3 portions and shape into loaves. Place in greased loaf pans 8½" x 4½", then place the pans in plastic bags to rise, until double in bulk, about 30 to 45 minutes.
8. Remove from bags. Punch down and remold loaves. Place in pans and return to bags. Let rise until double in bulk a second time.
9. Bake 30 to 40 minutes in preheated oven 350° F. to 375° F.
10. Remove from oven and let stand in pans 5 or 10 minutes. Turn out onto wire rack to cool.

# Monkey Bread

*Yield: Makes 1 pan (angel food or Bundt)*

### Cook's Corner

*Here's fun for the family to sit around the table, visiting and nibbling—like monkeys? This bread is already buttered. Nothing needs to be added.*

1 cup hot water
½ cup potato flakes, or ½ cup leftover mashed potatoes
¼ cup butter
1 cup buttermilk
1 tbsp active dry yeast
2 tbsps honey
2 eggs, well beaten
2 tsps salt
2 cups whole wheat flour
2 to 3 cups all-purpose flour
½ cup butter or margarine, melted for dipping

1. In a small bowl, beat potato flakes (or leftover mashed potatoes) into hot water with a wire whip. Add butter. Let cool.
2. In a small saucepan, heat buttermilk to 115° F. Remove from heat and add yeast and honey to dissolve.
3. Beat eggs well in large mixing bowl.

4. Add dissolved yeast mixture, potato, salt, and whole wheat flour. Beat vigorously 3 minutes.
5. Add 2 cups all-purpose flour and mix well.
6. Turn dough out onto well-floured surface and knead to a soft ball, adding more flour as needed to prevent sticking.
7. Let rise in mixer bowl about an hour.
8. Melt ½ cup butter in small saucepan.
9. Turn dough out onto floured surface and divide into 2 portions. Roll each into a rectangle about 15" x 13". With a pizza cutter, cut into strips ¾" wide. Then cut long strips crosswise into 3" pieces.
10. Dip each piece in melted butter and toss at random into a greased Bundt pan.
11. Let rise about 45-60 minutes or until double in bulk.
12. Bake about an hour at 375° F. to 400° F.
13. Remove from oven and let stand 5 to 10 minutes, then turn out onto a serving plate. Serve hot or cool. The fun of eating Monkey Bread is to break off the funny shapes.

**Tip:** If no Bundt pan is available and you must use a tube pan, if it is one with a bottom which separates, be sure to put a piece of foil on the bottom of the oven to catch the butter drippings which will seep out.

**Tip:** Dimalt is not very satisfactory in this recipe.

## VARIATION:

Another way of stacking the dough is to cut the 3" x ¾" pieces with the pizza cutter, dip them in butter, and stand them up lengthwise so that when baked, they will peel off almost in thick mini-slices.

*"Seconds count when dieting."*
Anonymous

# Anadama Bread

*Yield: 2 loaves*

### Cook's Corner

*This is a legendary, old-time bread, included in most bread books with many variations. So here is my adaptation. Legend has it that Anna baked the same bread recipe again and again from the time she was married. Finally, exasperated from the daily monotony, one night her husband threw a sack of cornmeal at Anna, exclaiming, "Anna, damn ya!" Instead of hitting Anna, the cornmeal splattered over the bread dough that was rising. Kneading it in, she baked the bread that way. The result is a delicious yeast cornbread.*

¼ cup warm water
1 tbsp active dry yeast
¼ tsp sugar
2 cups milk
½ cup yellow cornmeal
1 ½ tsps salt
⅓ cup light molasses
3 tbsps butter
3 ½ to 4 cups sifted all-purpose flour

1. In a small bowl or cup, sprinkle yeast and sugar over water. Let yeast dissolve.
2. In a large saucepan, immediately combine milk, cornmeal, and salt. Heat to boiling point, stirring constantly. Reduce to low heat and continue to cook 5 minutes, still stirring. It becomes thick like cornmeal mush.
3. Remove from heat. Add butter and molasses, stirring to melt the butter. Cool the mixture to 115° F.
4. Add yeast mixture and stir well. Add 3 cups of the sifted flour and turn out dough onto floured kneading surface. Knead 8 to 10 minutes, adding flour as necessary to prevent sticking. Do not knead in any more flour than is really necessary, which may leave up to a cup.
5. Return dough to the saucepan. Cover with plastic wrap and let rise until double in bulk, about 1 hour.
6. Turn out dough again onto lightly floured

*Facing page:* Caramel Cluster Pull-Aparts (p. 40)
*Following page:* Della's Cardamom Christmas Tree (p. 43); Louise's Raised Doughnuts (p. 59)

surface. Divide in half. Cover and let rest 10 minutes.

7. Shape into 2 loaves. Place in greased loaf pans 8½" x 4½". Lightly grease the tops, cover with plastic wrap, and let rise until double in bulk.

8. Bake 45 to 50 minutes at 375° F. to 400° F.

9. Remove from the oven and let stand 5 or 10 minutes in pans before turning out on wire rack to cool.

# German Fruit Bread (Hutzelbrot)

*Yield: 3 loaves*

### Cook's Corner

*Hutzel is the German word for wrinkled fruit (dried fruit). Here is another way to use a combination of dried fruits, as well as a way to salvage old dried fruit that may be dark and brittle. After baking, wrap tightly and refrigerate for at least two days for flavors to mellow. Or freeze it. Toasted for breakfast, it's especially delicious. You may want to slice the loaves before freezing and remove only the slices needed for a meal.*

4 cups assorted dried fruits (apples, apricots, peaches, pears, plums, cherries)
1 cup apple juice
1½ cups warm water
2 tbsps active dry yeast
½ cup honey
2 eggs, beaten
2 tsps salt
1 tsp ground cloves
1 tsp ground cardamom
1 tsp caraway seeds
1 tsp anise flavoring
½ cup wheat germ
½ cup vegetable oil
about 7 cups all-purpose flour
1 cup dates, coarsely cut
1 cup nuts, coarsely chopped

1. With scissors, snip dried fruit coarsely into a mixing bowl and set aside. (If fruit is very dry, first pour 1½ cups boiling water over it and let it stand 3 or 4 minutes. Drain. Then snip with scissors.)

2. Put warm water in a small mixing bowl and sprinkle yeast over it. Add honey. Let yeast dissolve.

3. Heat apple juice and pour over dried fruit in mixing bowl. Set aside. Juice will be completely absorbed.

4. Beat eggs in a large mixer bowl and add yeast mixture, salt, spices, flavorings, wheat germ, and oil.

5. Stir all together and beat in 3½ cups flour. Beat at medium speed 5 minutes.

6. With a slotted or wooden spoon, gradually beat in 2½ cups more flour.

7. Turn out dough onto floured kneading surface and knead until a soft, smooth ball is formed, adding flour only as necessary.

8. Return dough to mixer bowl. Cover with plastic wrap and let rise in a warm place until double in bulk, about 1½ hours.

9. Cut dates and nuts coarsely and stir into the fruit mixture.

10. Turn out dough onto a lightly floured surface and knead gently. Roll to a circle about ½ inch thick. Spread about half the fruit mixture over half of the dough and knead gently, pulling the dough over the fruit, then gradually working it through the dough. Add flour as needed to prevent sticking badly. Try to keep dough as soft as possible for a better bread.

11. Flatten other half of dough and add remaining fruit, working in as before.

12. Shape into 3 loaves and place in pans 8½" x 4½". Cover and let rise until double in bulk, about 1 hour.

13. Lightly oil tops of loaves. Bake 1 hour at 300° F. to 325° F. or until bread tests done when rapped with knuckles.

    During baking, place a piece of foil over the loaves to keep pieces of fruit on top from becoming brittle. Remove foil last 15 minutes so bread will brown nicely.

14. Remove loaves from oven and turn out on wire rack to cool.

—From Dora D. Flack, *Dry and Save* (Salt Lake City: Bookcraft, 1976), pp. 57-58.

*Facing page:* Italian Bread Sticks (p. 56), Pocket Bread (p. 57), and Soft Pretzels (p. 57), all from Lilian's Basic Specialty Bread Dough (p. 55)
*Preceding page:* Croissants (p. 49)

# Yeast Rolls and Specialties

(For an explanation of any unfamiliar ingredients listed in these recipes, see the discussion on Ingredients in the last section of this book.)

## Mother's Parker House Rolls

(See photograph on page 24)

*Yield: About 3 dozen large rolls*

### Cook's Corner

*With these rolls, Mother always said, "Easy does it. Handle gently. Don't press down hard with the rolling pin." Her rolls were almost as light as air.*

2 cups milk, scalded
2 tbsps active dry yeast
⅓ cup water (115° F.)
6 tbsps butter
¼ cup sugar
2 tsps salt
3 eggs, beaten *well*
5 to 6 cups all-purpose flour
about ¼ cup butter, melted for dipping dough

1. In small saucepan, scald milk.
2. In small bowl, dissolve yeast in ⅓ cup warm water.
3. Remove milk from burner when tiny bubbles begin to form.
4. To scalded milk, add butter, sugar, and salt; let cool to 115° F.
5. In large mixer bowl, beat eggs very well and add milk mixture, yeast, and 2 cups flour, beating *well*.
6. Add 2 more cups flour and beat again.
7. With wooden or slotted spoon, stir in 1 cup more flour, then add the last cup of flour, beating with spoon. Dough will be thick but sticky.
8. Cover bowl and set aside to rise in a warm place, about 2 hours, stirring down every time dough reaches top of bowl.
9. Melt butter and also butter baking pan 9″ x 13″.
10. On well-floured pastry cloth turn out dough and barely knead it. *Lightly* roll into a circle with dough about 3/8″ thick.
11. Cut with round cutter. Dip about half the circle in butter and fold over like a purse (butter will be inside) so top edge slightly overlaps the bottom. Place on baking sheet not too far apart. As the rolls rise, they will push together slightly and will rise up instead of out.
12. Bake 15 to 20 minutes at 400° F. to 425° F. or until lightly brown.
13. Remove carefully from pan and serve piping hot.

**Tip:** If you want to give an extra appeal to a perfectly delicious roll, add ½ to 1 tsp ginger. Experiment to see which you prefer, then write it on the recipe.

## Cinnamon Rolls

*Yield: About 18 rolls*

Using Mother's Parker House Rolls recipe, for Cinnamon Rolls increase the sugar from ¼ to ½ cup. When dough has risen for 2 hours, proceed for Cinnamon Rolls with the following filling:

1 to 2 cups raisins
¼ cup butter, melted
½ cup sugar or brown sugar
2 tsps cinnamon
1 cup chopped nuts (optional)

1. Plump raisins by letting them stand in hot water in a small bowl while preparing the dough.
2. Melt butter in tiny saucepan and grease 3 cookie sheets.
3. Combine sugar and cinnamon in a cup.
4. Chop nuts.
5. On pastry cloth, roll dough into a rectangle to about ¼ inch thick.
6. Spread dough with melted butter and sprinkle with sugar-cinnamon mixture.
7. Squeeze water from raisins and sprinkle over the dough with nuts.
8. Roll dough as for a jelly roll. With a string about a foot long, cut off ¾-inch slices by pulling the string under the roll with an end in each hand. Bring the string up and cross it, thus cutting the slices with precision and without collapsing the roll. Cutting with a knife squashes the rolls; cutting with a string allows the rolls to rise in a lovely mound shape.
9. Carefully place each roll on a greased cookie sheet with sufficient room for rising between the slices. Let rise until double in bulk.
10. Bake 15 to 20 minutes at 400° F. to 425° F. or until nicely browned. While rolls are still hot, remove carefully from pan and cool on wire rack.

*"Home is heart."*
Val Camenish Wilcox
from the musical
"The Warm Place"

# Eve's Salvage Rolls

*Yield: About 4 dozen Parker House Rolls or 2 pans of Caramel Cluster Pull-Aparts*

### Cook's Corner

*Here is a wonderful way to use up buttermilk or old cottage cheese which may be a little sour-smelling, or old yogurt, or old sour cream; leftover mashed potatoes, or dried potato flakes are also good additions.*

*This is a good recipe to use as an alternative for filled Holiday Breads, described on pages 44 and 47.*

1 ½ cups water
¼ cup potato flakes or powder, or leftover mashed potatoes
1 ½ cups buttermilk (or one of the products listed in Cook's Corner—blend cottage cheese until smooth)
1 tbsp active dry yeast (2 tbsps hastens rising)
⅓ cup honey or sugar
¼ cup shortening or butter
2 eggs, well beaten
5 cups all-purpose flour
2 tsps salt
2 to 3 cups more all-purpose flour

1. Boil water in medium-sized saucepan. Add potato flakes or mashed potatoes to water in saucepan and beat with slotted spoon until smooth.
2. Add buttermilk (or whatever), yeast, and sweetening to potato mixture in saucepan.
3. As yeast softens and begins to dissolve in saucepan, add butter. It will soften but not melt, in the warm mixture.
4. In small mixer bowl, beat eggs well and pour into large mixer bowl.
5. To eggs in large bowl add mixture in saucepan, together with salt and 5 cups flour, 1 cup at a time, beating *well* with electric mixer after each addition.
6. Dough will now be too stiff to continue beating with beaters. Using a slotted spoon, beat in another cup of flour gradually and turn out onto well-floured pastry cloth. Knead, adding only enough flour to prevent sticking, until a soft, smooth ball is formed.

7. Dust bowl and hands lightly with flour; work off residue of dough from hands and bowl and return the ball of dough to the large mixer bowl.

8. Cover with plastic wrap and let rise about 45 minutes to an hour, until double in bulk.

9. Turn out onto floured pastry cloth; roll and form into desired shapes—for example, Parker House or Crescents. This is a good all-round roll recipe.

10. Place on buttered baking sheets. Let rise until double in bulk.

11. Bake 15 to 20 minutes at 375° F. to 400° F.

# Caramel Cluster Pull-Aparts

(See photograph on page 33)

---

*Yield: Makes 2 pans (angel food or Bundt)*

---

### Cook's Corner

*What fun for the family or guests to sit around the table and informally enjoy these tasty pull-aparts, which are baked in a tube pan or a Bundt pan.*

Use your favorite roll recipe. Eve's Salvage Rolls and Mother's Parker House Rolls are both excellent for this. Each of those recipes makes 2 pans of Pull-Aparts. So if you want only one pan of Pull-Aparts, cut the roll recipe in half. Or use one pan straight from the oven and freeze another pan for unexpected guests. Or use half the roll recipe for conventional dinner rolls and make a pan of Pull-Aparts for a special dessert. Or refrigerate part of the dough for use the next day.

For each *half* of the recipe (one pan of Pull-Aparts), use the following dip mix and instructions:

½ cup butter, melted for dipping
1 cup brown sugar
1 cup finely chopped nuts (almonds chopped in the blender are great)
½ package of butterscotch instant pudding mix (3 5/8 oz. pkg.)

1. Melt butter in small saucepan.

2. Chop nuts. Mix together the nuts, brown sugar, and pudding mix in a small mixing bowl.

3. Divide risen dough into two portions, working with only one at a time. On floured pastry cloth, roll dough into a rectangle about 15″ x 8″. With pizza cutter, cut rectangle of dough into long strips about 1 inch wide. Then cut crosswise about every two inches. This will give you about 48 small pieces. This is much quicker and easier than rolling dough into balls.

4. Dip each piece first in melted butter, then roll in sugar-nut-pudding mixture.

5. Place loosely in lightly buttered angel food pan or Bundt pan. Cover the bottom of the pan with the balls, then continue laying in more balls until pieces are all stacked loosely in the pan. Do not crowd or press together. The pan will be about half full. Sprinkle residue mixture over top of dough pieces. Let rise about 45 minutes, no more than double in bulk.

6. Bake 30 to 40 minutes on bottom rack at 350° F. to 375° F.

   Some guests prefer a well-baked roll, while others prefer a very soft, almost underdone roll. With this recipe you can cater to both tastes by paying strict attention to your method of baking. Place the pan on the middle rack and the top layer of pull-aparts will be crisp while the bottom remains very soft.

7. Let cool 5 or 10 minutes before turning upside down onto serving plate. Best when served hot.

**Tip:** These can be reheated. Preheat oven to 375° F. Place rolls in large paper sack. Sprinkle the sack with water. Close the opening. Leave in the oven 15 or 20 minutes with heat turned off.

**Caution:** Be careful to fill the pan so that it is not more than half full or so that it does not rise too high, thus preventing butter and sugar from spilling over and burning in the oven.

# Special Dinner Party Rolls

## (To be mixed day or morning before baking)

*Yield: About 3 dozen rolls*

2 tbsps yeast
½ cup warm water
½ cup boiling water
½ cup butter (no substitute)
1 cup cold water
4 to 5 cups sifted whole wheat flour
1 ½ tsps salt
3 eggs, beaten
½ cup brown sugar or honey

1. In a cup or small bowl, sprinkle the yeast over the water. Let yeast dissolve.
2. In a small saucepan, boil ½ cup water and add butter. Let butter melt, then add 1 cup cold water.
3. Sift the flour and salt together twice and set aside.
4. In large mixer bowl, beat eggs well. Add yeast and sweetening.
5. Add sifted dry ingredients, beating 3 to 5 minutes on medium to high speed. This will be a very sticky dough.
6. Cover with plastic wrap and let rise in the same bowl until double. Stir down and place in refrigerator.
7. Stir down several times as it continues to rise. You will notice that it becomes stiffer through these repeated stirrings.
8. About 2 ½ hours before serving time, remove dough from refrigerator. The soft dough is easier to handle when cold because it isn't as sticky. Knead slightly on floured board and divide into 3 portions for convenient handling.
9. Shape into the type of rolls desired. Let rise about 2 hours or until double in bulk.
10. Bake 12 to 15 minutes at 400° F. to 425° F.
11. Remove from oven and serve piping hot.

—From Vernice G. Rosenvall, Mabel H. Miller, and Dora D. Flack, *Wheat for Man: Why and How*, 3rd ed. (Salt Lake City: Bookcraft, 1975), p. 35.

# Eve's Knot Buns

(See photograph on page 24)

*Yield: 3 dozen*

## Cook's Corner

*These buns are a favorite with the Bean family. When Eve's young son watched her making the knots one day, he said, "Mom, when I grow up and get a wife, will you teach her how to make these buns?"*

2 cups milk, scalded
2 tbsps active dry yeast
½ cup warm water
¼ tsp sugar
½ cup butter
1 tsp salt
4 tbsps sugar
2 eggs, well beaten
5 to 6 cups all-purpose flour

## For Dipping:

1 ¼ cups sugar
3 tbsps cinnamon
1 cup margarine or butter, melted

1. In a large saucepan (about 3-quart), scald milk.
2. In a small bowl, set yeast to dissolve in warm water with pinch of sugar.
3. In small mixer bowl, beat eggs well.
4. Stir butter, salt, and sugar into hot milk and place in cold water in the sink to cool.
5. To mixture in saucepan add beaten eggs, dissolved yeast, and 2 cups flour. Beat well with slotted spoon.
6. Cover with plastic wrap and let rise about 30 minutes in the saucepan.
7. Add enough flour (approximately 3 to 4 cups) to make a soft dough, beating with slotted spoon. Turn out onto floured surface and knead 5 minutes.
8. Cover with plastic wrap and let rise about 1 hour.
9. In a small mixing bowl, combine sugar and cinnamon for dipping.
10. Melt butter.
11. Grease muffin tins.

12. Roll out dough about 5/8 inch thick. With pizza cutter, cut into long strips 2 inches wide. Then cut crosswise to make strips 2 inches wide and 5 inches long.

13. Dip each strip in melted butter, then sugar-cinnamon mixture.

14. Tie each strip loosely in overhand knot, as if you are starting to tie your shoe, and place in lightly greased muffin tins.

15. Let rise 30 minutes and bake 10 to 15 minutes at 375° F. to 400° F. or until golden brown. Remove from tins while still warm so they won't stick. Delicious when served piping hot or cool.

**Tip:** If 3 muffin tins are not available, use what you have and finish the rest of the knots by placing them on greased cookie sheets like butterhorns. Let rise and bake as above.

## VARIATION:

This recipe also makes delicious dinner rolls. Eliminate the sugar and cinnamon and simply dip the strips in melted butter, tie the knot and bake as explained in the above tip.

# *Buttermilk Butterhorns*

(See photograph on page 24)

*Yield: 2 dozen*

2 cups buttermilk
2 tbsps active dry yeast
½ cup sugar or brown sugar
½ cup butter
4 eggs, well beaten
2 cups whole wheat flour
2 ½ to 3 cups all-purpose flour
2 tsps salt
½ tsp baking soda
about ¼ cup butter for spreading on roll dough

1. In medium-sized saucepan, heat buttermilk to 115° F.

2. Add yeast and sugar to warm buttermilk and let yeast activate.

3. While yeast is dissolving, beat eggs in large mixer bowl.

4. Add butter to buttermilk mixture to soften butter.

5. Sift together whole wheat flour, salt, and soda.

6. To beaten eggs add yeast-buttermilk mixture and sifted dry ingredients. Beat 5 minutes at medium to high speed. Let rest 10 minutes.

7. Add remaining dry ingredients and beat well with slotted or wooden spoon. If necessary, add ½ cup more flour to make a soft dough.

8. Refrigerate at least 4 hours, preferably all day or overnight, stirring down occasionally.

9. About 2 hours before serving time, remove dough from refrigerator. Punch down and turn out onto floured surface. Knead slightly.

10. Divide dough into 3 portions. Roll the first portion into a circle about 8 inches in diameter. Follow the same procedure with each portion.

11. Melt ¼ cup butter and spread with hand or pastry brush all over the circle.

12. Cut the circle into 8 wedge-shaped pieces, like you do a pie. Starting at the wide end, roll each wedge loosely so that the roll builds up higher in the middle part.

13. Place on greased baking sheets, leaving room between the rolls for rising. Let rise about an hour before baking.

14. Bake 12 to 15 minutes at 375° F. to 400° F. or until golden brown. Serve piping hot.

*"Who learns and learns
But acts not what he knows,
Is one who plows and plows
But never sows."*
Oriental proverb

# Della's Cardamom Christmas Tree (Basic Holiday Bread)

(See photograph on page 34)

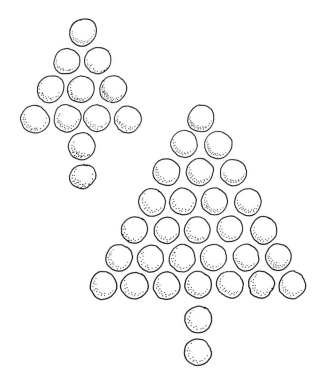

*Yield: 2 large trees, 4 smaller trees, or a variable number as desired, depending on size and number of balls used.*

1 ½ cups milk
2 tbsps active dry yeast
½ cup warm water (115° F.)
¼ tsp sugar
½ cup sugar
¾ cup shortening
2 tsps salt
3 eggs
¾ to 1 tsp cardamom
about 5 ½ to 6 ½ cups all-purpose flour

1. In a medium-sized saucepan, scald milk.
2. In a small bowl or cup, sprinkle yeast and ¼ tsp sugar over ½ cup warm water. Let yeast dissolve.
3. When milk is scalded, remove from burner and add sugar, shortening, and salt. Speed cooling by placing pan in the sink with cool water for a few minutes.
4. In large mixer bowl, beat eggs and add yeast mixture, milk mixture, and cardamom. Add 3 cups all-purpose flour and beat for 3 minutes on medium to high speed.
5. With slotted spoon, stir in more flour until stiff enough to turn out onto floured pastry cloth. Knead, adding flour as necessary to prevent sticking until a soft, elastic ball is formed.
6. Return dough to mixer bowl and let rise until double in bulk.
7. For large trees (for big families or for guests), grease 2 large cookie sheets. Punch down dough and turn out onto pastry cloth. Divide in half. From each half, form 30 balls, 1 ½″ round. (I cut them with a pizza cutter for uniformity, then form into balls.) Only a large 17″ x 14″ sheet will accommodate 30 balls.

8. Here's how to build the tree: Near the bottom of the cookie sheet and in the middle of the width, place 2 balls, one above the other for the trunk. In a line across the width of the sheet, just above the trunk, arrange 7 balls. Place the balls barely apart to allow for rising. Add 6 for the next row, fitting balls into the niches of the bottom row. Don't press the balls together; leave them barely apart for rising room. Now build the rest of the tree, diminishing each row by one ball until the last ball becomes the tip.
9. Cover with plastic wrap and let rise until double in bulk, usually about 30 to 45 minutes, depending on room temperature.
10. Bake on bottom rack of preheated oven 12 to 15 minutes at 375° F. to 400° F. or until golden brown.
11. Remove from oven and let stand in pan 5 to 10 minutes. *Very* carefully remove with spatula to serving tray. An open-ended cookie sheet is helpful.
12. Frost with butter icing. Decorate as desired with colored sugar or multicolored balls or with candied fruits to look like ornaments.

**BUTTER ICING** (For optional icing on trees or on Holiday Breads following this recipe):

3 cups powdered sugar

¼ cup butter

4 tbsps plus 1 tsp canned milk

In a medium-sized mixing bowl, combine ingredients and beat well. This will ice two large trees. Don't load the tree with icing. Use a small spatula to better cover the roundness of the balls. *Or*, using a decorator tube, drizzle icing over the tree, decorating as desired. Cover with a towel if tree is not to be served almost immediately. Plastic wrap sometimes makes it sweat. If freezing trees for later use, wrap well in plastic wrap or aluminum foil, then ice and decorate when thawed.

**Tip:** These are *big* trees, filling a large cookie sheet to the edges, and each ball is generously large. I prefer making 4 trees instead of 2, with the balls only half as big. Or make them any desired size, down to 3 balls across the bottom row above the trunk (one ball for the trunk). This tiny tree requires only 7 balls. Using the same basic construction, you can make any size between the tiny and the big tree. Have fun!

**Tip:** This basic Holiday Bread dough is superb for any type of roll. Use half whole wheat for a change. Delicious! You might want to leave out the cardamom and substitute 1 tsp cinnamon or nutmeg or ginger.

**Tip:** This dough makes appealing "Russian" loaves. Use a 16-oz. vegetable can (for small loaves) or a 3-lb. shortening can (for large loaves). Grease cans well and fill half full with ball of dough. Let rise barely above top of rim. During baking it will rise higher and make a top ball resembling a Russian mosque. Decorate as desired.

# Holiday Breads: Ladder Roll

*Yield: 4 ladders*

Use Della's Basic Holiday Bread recipe (or Eve's Salvage Roll recipe on page 39) and proceed as follows:

1. Roll a quarter portion of the basic recipe into an oblong 15″ x 6″.
2. Place this sheet of dough on a greased cookie sheet.
3. Choose one of the fillings on page 48 and spoon it down the center, leaving a good 1½″ of uncovered dough on each side.
4. With scissors, about every 2″ down the length of the dough oblong, cut from the edge of the dough toward the filling. Make 7 or 8 cuts on each side along the whole length of the oblong.
5. Bring matching strips of dough from opposite sides to the center, crossing the strips over the filling.
6. Bake as directed in Della's Basic Holiday Bread recipe. To be sure "filled" bread is fully baked, add about 10 minutes to baking time. To avoid excessive browning on top, slip a sheet of aluminum foil over the roll during last half of baking time.

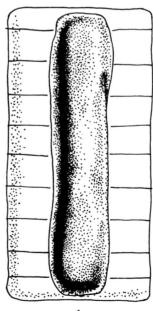

1

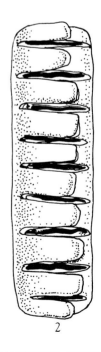

2

*Facing page:* Crackers (p. 61); Rye Wafers (p. 61); Graham Crackers (p. 61)

# Holiday Breads: Candy Cane

*Yield: 3 or 4 canes, depending on desired size*

Use Della's Basic Holiday Bread recipe (or Eve's Salvage Roll recipe on page 39) and proceed as follows:

1. Divide dough into 3 or 4 portions, as desired. Proceed as if making a Ladder Roll, using canned cherry pie filling.
2. Gently turn the top of the roll to resemble the curve of a candy cane. With imagination, the strips, crossed over the red, resemble stripes.
3. Bake as directed in Della's Basic Holiday Bread recipe. To be sure "filled" bread is fully baked, add about 10 minutes to baking time. To avoid excessive browning on top, slip a sheet of aluminum foil over the canes during last half of baking time.

This roll can be frosted, if desired, but I prefer lightly sifting a little powdered sugar over it or leaving it plain. Or decorate it with candied fruit, as desired.

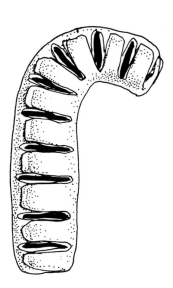

# Holiday Breads: Swedish Tea Ring

*Yield: 2 or 3 tea rings, depending on desired size*

Use Della's Basic Holiday Bread recipe (or Eve's Salvage Roll recipe on page 39) and proceed as follows:

1. Choose one of the fillings on page 48. Roll out the oblong of dough and spread with filling.
2. Roll as for a jelly roll and form into a ring.
3. Place on greased cookie sheet.
4. With scissors, cut from the outer edge toward the center, halfway through. Twist the little cut half slices upward so that the filling shows. If desired, a maraschino or candied cherry can be placed in each upturned half circle.
5. Bake as directed in Della's Basic Holiday Bread recipe. To be sure "filled" bread is fully baked, add about 10 minutes to baking time. To avoid excessive browning on top, slip a sheet of aluminum foil over the rings during last half of baking time.

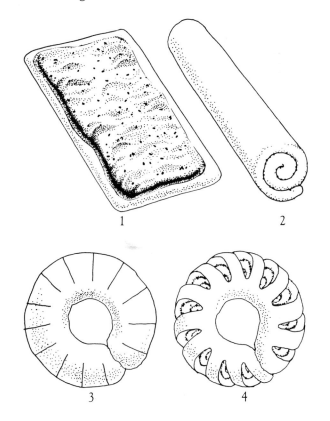

*Facing page:* Banana Bread (p. 65); Myrtle's Pumpkin Bread (p. 66); Pumpkin Muffins (p. 67)

# Fillings for Holiday Breads

## FILLING #1, Date or Raisin

*Yield: 1 tea ring or 2 ladders*

1 cup raisins or chopped dates
1 tbsp brown sugar
½ tsp cornstarch
⅓ cup water
½ cup chopped nuts (pecans, walnuts, or almonds)
1 tbsp lemon juice

1. Combine fruit, sugar, cornstarch, water, and nuts; cook, stirring constantly, 3 to 5 minutes, until it reaches a spreading consistency.
2. Remove from heat and add lemon juice. Stir well and cool.

## FILLING #2, Apricot

*Yield: 2 rolls*

2 cups dried apricots (11-oz. pkg)
1 cup boiling water
¼ cup butter or margarine
1 cup sugar
1 tbsp lemon juice
1 cup chopped nuts (walnuts, pecans, or almonds)
dash of nutmeg

1. With scissors, cut apricots into large pieces.
2. In a small saucepan, pour boiling water over apricots. Let stand 5 minutes, then simmer about 15 minutes.
3. Add butter to apricot mixture and stir until melted.
4. Add sugar and lemon juice. Stir well.
5. Add nuts and nutmeg.

**Tip:** This is prettier with commercially dried apricots than with home-dried apricots, which are usually darker in color.

## FILLING #3, Cherry or Apple or Blueberry or Pineapple

*Yield: 1 can makes 1 tea ring or 2 ladders*

When using commercial canned filling, I stir in 1 tbsp melted butter and ½ tsp cinnamon to heighten flavor, and proceed as with other filling.

## FILLING #4, Sugar and Cinnamon

*Yield: 1 tea ring or 2 ladders*

2 tbsps butter, melted
½ cup brown sugar
1 tsp cinnamon
½ cup chopped nuts of your choice

1. In a small mixing bowl, combine sugar, cinnamon, and nuts. Set aside.
2. Spread melted butter over oblong of dough.
3. Sprinkle dry ingredients over melted butter and roll as directed previously.

# Lois's Orange Delight Rolls

*Yield: 2 dozen*

1 cup milk, scalded
½ cup sugar
2 tbsps butter
1 tbsp active dry yeast
3 eggs
1 cup all-purpose flour
3 cups all-purpose flour
1 tsp salt

1. In a small saucepan, scald milk. Remove from burner. Pour into large mixer bowl. Add sugar and butter; this will melt butter and cool milk.
2. When milk is down to 115° F., add yeast and let it dissolve.
3. Beat eggs on high speed until very fluffy. Add to milk mixture with 1 cup flour. Beat well.

4. Let batter rise at room temperature 1 to 2 hours.

5. Sift together 3 times the remaining 3 cups flour and salt. Add to above mixture, beating well with a slotted spoon.

6. Let rise in bowl until double in bulk.

7. Turn out onto generously floured pastry cloth. Knead until it forms a very soft dough.

8. Divide into two portions. Roll each half, one at a time, ¼" thick. Spread with filling (below). Roll as for jelly roll.

9. Cut with string or heavy thread into 24 slices. (Cutting with string avoids mashing the slices. Slide string under the roll, leaving a ½" to 1" slice. Holding the string ends with both hands, pull them up and cross the string and it will cut the slice.)

10. Place slices in buttered muffin cups. Cover with plastic wrap and let rise double in bulk.

11. Bake 10 to 15 minutes at 400° F. to 425° F. May be frosted if desired.

## Filling:

½ cup sugar
6 tbsps butter, softened
rind of 1 orange, grated
Cream all ingredients together to a spreading consistency.

## Frosting:

1 cup powdered sugar
½ cup orange juice
Mix together. Pour over warm rolls.

**Tip:** Refrigerate dough overnight, if necessary, then proceed with rolling and forming rolls. Of course, cold dough takes longer to rise. Cover with plastic wrap. Let rise and bake as above.

**Tip:** When you have quite a few leftover orange rinds, put them through your food processor, then freeze in plastic bags for future use. If you do not have a food processor, freeze the rinds (they will not become rigid) and grate on a hand grater. These can also be frozen in plastic bags for future use.

# Croissants

(See photograph on page 35)

*Yield: 2 ½ to 3 dozen, depending on size*

## Cook's Corner

*Most people stumble over the pronunciation of this word; the dictionary gives it as "krwaSAANZ."*

*Although this flaky pastry-like roll is attributed to the French, it actually originated in Budapest in 1686 when Budapest was under siege by the Turks. At last the Turks decided to take the town by tunneling under the city walls. However, they were unaware that the industrious bakers worked all night in order to have the staff of life fresh and tempting for the townspeople every morning. As the bakers worked, they heard strange noises. Upon investigating, they discovered the reason and sounded an alarm which saved the city.*

*To commemorate the event, the bakers shaped a new pastry to resemble the crescent moon on the Turkish flag. This dough should be slammed and rolled, perhaps reflecting their ire against the would-be captors. Thus Croissants were born.*

*The simplified adaptation below—yes, it really is simplified even though the instructions are lengthy—is for one of those days you get to stay home, and it is truly worth the effort. You'll gain new respect from your guests as they savor each bite of these flaky rolls. Piping hot from the oven, they almost melt in the mouth; reheated, they are just as mouth-watering. And they are delicious even for snacking. Do try them!*

1 tbsp active dry yeast
6 tbsps warm water (115° F.)
4 cups all-purpose flour
2 tbsps sugar
1 tsp salt
1 to 1 ¼ cups milk
1 cup butter, chilled (no substitute, please)
1 egg, beaten for glaze

1. In a cup or small bowl, sprinkle yeast over the water. (You may need a pinch of sugar, but the yeast dissolves without it, only a little slower.) Let it stand 5 or 10 minutes to dissolve.

2. Sift flour, sugar, and salt together twice, for lightness.

3. Put about 1 cup of flour mixture in a small bowl and stir in yeast mixture. Add a bit more

flour if necessary to make it quite stiff and form into a ball.

4. Cut a cross in the top of the ball for better rising and drop the ball into a large bowl of warm water.

5. Sift remaining flour mixture into a large mixing bowl. With pastry blender, crumble ½ cup of the butter with the flour to resemble crumbs.

6. Mix in enough milk to make a dough that is soft, but not sticky. (A pastry cloth is most desirable at this point. Dough doesn't stick to the cloth as much as it does to a plain breadboard or tabletop.) Slam the doughy mass onto the lightly floured cloth. Slam about 5 minutes, adding a bit of flour only as needed. Slam longer if you have more frustrations to get rid of. This slamming develops the gluten and the dough will be smooth and elastic. (Now you'll know why you add so little flour at a time—because it does scatter with the slamming action.) Return the wonderful dough to the mixing bowl.

7. By the time you have finished this vigorous exercise, the yeast ball has risen to the surface of the water and is almost double in size—perhaps even more. Don't worry. Drain the ball with a slotted spoon and add to the dough in the mixing bowl.

8. Knead together thoroughly until you have another beautiful, smooth ball. Place dough in a bowl dusted with flour.

9. Cover with plastic wrap and let stand in refrigerator at least 2 to 3 hours. Or overnight is fine. If dough rises to the top of the bowl, just punch it down. Chilled dough is easy to handle and will be the same temperature as the butter. This is important.

10. Place remaining ½ cup butter between 2 sheets of waxed paper. With a rolling pin, press the butter until it is pliable but not sticky and is shaped into a 4-inch square pat. Return the butter, between the waxed paper, to the refrigerator.

11. Punch down dough and roll on pastry cloth to a 14″ x 5″ oblong shape.

12. Place half of the butter pat in the center third of the dough oblong. Fold one side of the dough (⅓ of the whole) over the butter. Place the remaining half of the butter pat on top of the fold of dough, then fold over the remaining end of the dough, making three layers of dough.

13. Turn the stack of dough so that one open end faces you. With the rolling pin, roll again into an oblong. You will see chunks of butter breaking and being distributed throughout the dough. Good! Repeat the rolling and folding into thirds.

14. Place this between the waxed paper which held the butter and lay it on a refrigerator shelf to chill 15 minutes or until firm.

15. Later on, after you have had more practice and you have become adept at rolling the dough, like the Budapest bakers, add up to ¼ cup more butter to make it even flakier.

16. Remove from the refrigerator and roll and fold the dough twice more. Return it to the refrigerator to chill again.

17. Remove from the refrigerator and again repeat rolling and folding. This thoroughly distributes the butter, making it a flakier roll.

18. Now you are ready to shape the Croissants. Roll out the dough to a large oblong, only 1/8 inch thick. This will more than cover the pastry cloth. Don't worry. You can still cut it properly.

19. With a pizza cutter, cut into 5- or 6-inch squares, cutting lengthwise of the whole oblong, then crosswise. Next cut the squares in half diagonally so that you have triangles.

20. Roll up, starting at the base of each triangle. Press down well the tip of the triangle.

21. Lightly flour cookie sheets, as many as you have. If you have leftover rolls, more than you have sheets for, just let them rise on the pastry cloth until a sheet is available for them after a pan has already baked. Just transfer them from the cloth to the pan very carefully so they won't collapse.

22. Place the rolled rolls on the cookie sheet, leaving room for rising in between them. Turn the two ends down, shaping the croissants like horseshoes. If crustier croissants are desired, flour the back of cookie sheets and bake croissants on the back so they get better hot air circulation.

23. Cover the rolls with plastic wrap and let them rise in a warm place for 20 to 25 minutes, or until almost doubled.
24. Pre-heat the oven to 425° F.
25. With a wire whip, beat the egg in a small bowl. Just before putting the croissants in the oven, brush the tops with a pastry brush dipped in beaten egg.
26. Bake 5 minutes at the high temperature. Turn down heat to 375° F. and bake 10 to 12 minutes longer, or until lightly browned.
27. Remove from oven and carefully lift off the croissants, with a spatula, to cool on wire racks.

**Tip:** These can be frozen for future use; they will taste like new when reheated. Preheat the oven to 375° F. Place croissants in a paper sack. Sprinkle sack with water and slip it into the oven. Turn off the heat and let them remain in the oven for about 15 minutes.

## VARIATION:

Dimalt can be used with this recipe. Substitute 2 tsps dimalt for the sugar. Add it with the yeast and be sure the water is no hotter than 110° F. Then proceed the same as outlined.

*QUICK & EASY*
# Buttermilk Scones

*Yield: 2 to 3 dozen*

2 cups buttermilk
4 tsps active dry yeast
½ cup warm water (115° F.)
5 to 6 cups all-purpose flour
1 tsp salt
½ tsp soda
2 tsp baking powder
2 eggs
¼ cup sugar
2 tbsps vegetable oil
oil for frying

1. In medium-sized saucepan, warm buttermilk to 115° F.
2. Dissolve yeast in ½ cup warm water.
3. Sift together 5 cups flour, salt, soda, and baking powder. Set aside.
4. Beat eggs in large mixing bowl and add sugar and oil.
5. To the egg mixture add buttermilk and dissolved yeast.
6. Immediately start adding sifted dry ingredients gradually, beating constantly. When batter starts to climb the beaters, start stirring with a slotted or wooden spoon, adding enough flour to make a soft dough.
7. Turn out onto generously floured kneading surface, preferably a pastry cloth. Roll out gently to about 5/8" thick.
8. With pizza cutter, cut dough into 2" x 4" rectangles or a little less. Let rise about 30 minutes on the cloth.
9. Heat oil to 350° F. to 375° F. in a deep-fat fryer. When oil is hot, start frying the scones, turning when bottom side is brown. While you are frying the scones, the dough on the cloth is still rising and you will have to use the pizza cutter again to separate the rectangles as they are to be fried.
10. Drain on paper towels and serve piping hot with butter and/or honey.

*"The two things of greatest value that we can give our children are roots and wings."*
Anonymous

# English Muffins

*Yield: 18 muffins*

### Cook's Corner

*In case of power emergency, these could be made on top of a coal- or wood-burning stove.*

1 cup milk, scalded
3 tbsps butter
1 tsp salt
2 tbsps sugar
1 tbsp active dry yeast
¼ cup warm water (115° F.)
¼ tsp sugar
1 egg, beaten
4 to 4 ½ cups all-purpose flour

1. Scald milk in 2-quart saucepan. Add butter, salt, and sugar. Set aside to cool to warm temperature.
2. In small bowl or a cup, set yeast to dissolve in ¼ cup warm water with ¼ tsp sugar.
3. Beat egg and add with yeast mixture to milk in saucepan.
4. Add flour gradually, beating with slotted spoon until stiff enough to turn out onto floured surface.
5. Knead a few minutes to make very soft elastic ball.
6. Return to saucepan, cover with plastic wrap and let rise about 1 hour.
7. Punch down. Roll dough ¼ inch thick. With round cookie cutter or a glass, cut in circles. Re-knead the scraps of dough between circles and cut more circles.
8. Sprinkle cookie sheet with cornmeal and place circles with space between for rising and spreading. Sprinkle tops with cornmeal.
9. Cover circles with plastic wrap and let rise about an hour.
10. Flour fingertips before carefully lifting light dough to griddle to prevent collapse of dough.
11. Bake on hot, ungreased griddle over low to medium heat 10 to 12 minutes per side (about 300° F. to 350° F.). Do not crowd on griddle and don't worry about the circles still rising. Just handle carefully and they will be all right.
12. Remove baked muffins to wire rack and let them cool.

**Tip:** These muffins can be frozen and then reheated for later use.

**Tip:** Delicious when sliced crosswise and toasted.

# Wheat English Muffins

*Yield: 18 muffins*

### Cook's Corner

*In case of power outage, these could be made on top of a coal- or wood-burning stove.*

1 tbsp active dry yeast
¼ cup warm water (115° F.)
¼ tsp sugar
1 cup buttermilk
3 tbsps butter
1 tsp salt
¼ tsp sugar
1 egg, beaten
¼ tsp baking soda
2 cups whole wheat flour
2 to 2 ½ cups all-purpose flour

1. In a small bowl or a cup, let yeast dissolve in ¼ cup water with ¼ tsp sugar.
2. In medium-sized saucepan, heat buttermilk to 115° F. and add butter, salt, and sugar. Remove from heat.
3. Beat egg and add with yeast mixture to buttermilk in saucepan.
4. Sift together whole wheat flour and soda and add gradually, beating with slotted spoon.
5. Add white flour gradually until stiff enough to turn out onto floured surface.
6. Knead a few minutes to a very soft, elastic ball.
7. Return dough to saucepan for rising. Cover with plastic wrap and let rise about 1 hour.
8. Punch down and roll dough to ¼ inch thick.
9. With round cookie cutter or drinking glass, cut

in circles. Re-knead the scraps of dough cut away from circles and cut more circles.

10. Sprinkle cookie sheets with cornmeal and place the circles on the cornmeal with space between for rising and spreading. Sprinkle tops with cornmeal.

11. Cover circles with plastic wrap. Let rise about 1 hour.

12. Flour fingertips before carefully lifting light dough to griddle to prevent collapse of dough.

13. Bake on hot, ungreased griddle over low to medium heat 10 to 15 minutes per side. Do not crowd on griddle and don't worry about the circles still rising. Just handle carefully and they will be all right.

14. Remove baked muffins to wire rack and let them cool.

**Tip:** These muffins can be frozen and then re-heated for later use.

# Bread Sticks

*Yield: About 3 dozen*

1 cup warm water (115°F.)
1 tbsp active dry yeast
2 tbsps sugar
1 tsp salt
¼ cup oil
2½ to 3 cups all-purpose flour or whole wheat flour
1 egg, for glazing

1. Pour water into medium-sized mixing bowl. Sprinkle yeast and sugar into water. Let yeast dissolve.

2. Add salt and oil to liquid and 1 cup of flour gradually, beating vigorously with a slotted spoon. Add flour as necessary until a soft ball is formed that can be turned out onto a floured kneading surface.

3. Knead 5 minutes, adding only enough flour to make a soft dough.

4. Return dough to mixing bowl and let rise 1 hour until double in bulk.

5. Punch down and turn out onto floured surface. Divide into 2 portions. Do not knead because this makes it harder to roll out the dough.

6. With a rolling pin, roll each ball, one at a time, into an oblong about 3/8 inch thick.

7. With a wire whip, beat the egg in a small mixing bowl.

8. With a pastry brush, coat the dough with egg. Sprinkle with sesame seed and/or seasoning salt as desired.

9. With a pizza cutter, cut the dough the length of the rectangle in strips about 3/8 inch wide. Then cut crosswise in the middle for easier handling.

10. Carefully lift the strips and place them about ¼ inch apart on the greased backs of 2 cookie sheets, being careful not to stretch the dough.

11. Let rise about 20 minutes.

12. Bake on middle rack of oven about 20 minutes at 375° F. to 400° F. For more crustiness, bake a little longer at a lower temperature.

13. When sticks are golden brown, remove from oven and cool on wire racks. These soften right after baking. If you want them to stay soft, store in a plastic bag. If you want sticks to stay crisp and hard, keep them in the air if you do not live in a humid climate. If necessary, crisp them by putting them on a cookie sheet and leaving them in a preheated oven (350° F.) about 5 minutes.

## VARIATIONS:

1. Dimalt can be used as a sugar substitute. Use 1 tsp dimalt sprinkled over yeast and let it work with the yeast as it activates. Leave out the sugar.

2. Spread rectangle of dough with melted butter. Sprinkle with Parmesan or American dried grated cheese.

Or sprinkle on cheese without butter.

Or use Lemon 'n Herb or any seasoning salt desired.

Or cut each portion and roll with palms of hands on kneading surface to form individual sticks. The method first described, however, is much quicker.

# Vivian's Pizza

*Yield: 3 pizzas*

### Cook's Corner

*Here is a pizza that is tops in economy and convenience. Cube and freeze leftover bits of ham, turkey, pork roast, or other meat. Add other toppings listed below and you have pizza in a hurry at a fraction of the cost of the commercial product.*

## DOUGH:
1 cup warm water
1 tbsp active dry yeast
1 tsp sugar
1 tsp salt
1 tbsp shortening
3 cups all-purpose flour

1. In a small bowl, dissolve yeast in warm water with sugar.
2. Into a medium-sized mixing bowl sift salt and flour.
3. With pastry blender, cut shortening into flour mixture to make crumbs as with pie crust.
4. Add dissolved yeast mixture to crumbs and knead thoroughly.
5. Let rise an hour.
6. On floured surface, roll out thin into three circles and press into pizza pans, working dough to the edges. This will fill 3 large round pizza pans.
7. Let rise 30 minutes before putting toppings on the pizza.
8. These pizza crusts can be frozen in the pans, then removed, wrapped in plastic wrap and kept frozen for later use. Remove from freezer a few minutes before using and arrange toppings over the dough. Bake as above.

## TOPPING #1:
1 8-oz. can tomato sauce
1 tsp oregano, ground
meat cubes, as desired
cheese, as desired

1. Combine sauce and oregano and spread on pizza dough.
2. Sprinkle generously with ham cubes, pepperoni, Canadian bacon, olives, green pepper, pineapple, mushrooms, etc. (use your imagination).
3. Top with cheese as desired—mild, sharp, jack, mozzarella.
4. Bake about 15 minutes at 400° F. to 425° F.
5. Cut in wedges and serve piping hot.

## TOPPING #2 (Dora's family favorite):
2 pounds ground beef
2 tbsps dried onion
1 can tomato soup
salt and pepper to taste
oregano, a few shakes as desired
cheese (mozzarella and medium sharp), as
    desired

1. Soak onion in 2 tbsps of water.
2. Brown beef in frying pan and add onion.
3. Add tomato soup and cook a few minutes.
4. Spread meat sauce over crusts (this is enough for all three crusts) and sprinkle with oregano.
5. Top with grated cheese as desired.
6. Sprinkle grated parmesan cheese over the top, if desired.
7. Bake 20 to 30 minutes at 400° F. to 425° F.
8. Cut in wedges and serve piping hot.

**Tip:** Sometimes for my big family I cook this on a big cookie sheet and cut into squares for serving.

**Tip:** Topping #2 is sufficient to cover 3 round pizzas. This topping can be cooked, then part of it frozen according to your specific need. Thaw as needed and spread on a frozen pizza crust. Add cheeses and bake.

# Lilian's Basic Specialty Bread Dough

### Cook's Corner

*Lilian DeLong conducts the Tradewinds Cooking Schools, 293 East 1100 North, Centerville, UT 84014, phone (801) 295-5512. She has shared the following Basic Specialty Bread Dough recipe and her recipes and ideas are used with her permission, but I am adapting them to fit my format.*

*From this basic recipe you can make excellent French bread, Italian breadsticks, pocket bread, pretzels, bagels, pizza, and hot dog and hamburger buns.*

2 cups warm water
1 tbsp active dry yeast
2 tbsps sugar
2 tsps salt
5 to 6 cups all-purpose flour

1. Pour warm water into large mixing bowl of the bread mixer. Sprinkle in yeast and sugar and let yeast dissolve.
2. Add 5 cups flour and the salt and knead 8 to 10 minutes. Use this recipe for any or all of the following products.

This dough is superior when kneaded in the bread mixer but can be done by hand.

# French Bread

(See photograph on page 23)

*Yield: 2 loaves*

Use Lilian's Basic Specialty Bread Dough above and proceed as follows:

1. Cover dough and let rise until double in bulk.
2. Punch down and let rise a second time in bowl.
3. Punch down and divide into two portions. Shape into 2 long oblong rolls.
4. Place in rising cradles, cover, and let rise double in bulk.
5. In the oven preheat unglazed quarry tiles or a ceramic stone to 400° F. Also place a shallow pan of water with a brick set in it on the bottom of the oven.
6. Pull oven rack out as far as possible so you won't be burned as you generously sprinkle cornmeal on the tiles. If using rising cradles, gently roll dough onto cornmeal-coated tiles. Allow room between the loaves for rising during baking. Quickly slash the tops diagonally with a sharp knife or a razor blade.
7. Sprinkle with poppy seed or sesame seed if desired.
8. Generously spray the loaves with water before sliding the rack back in place and closing the oven door.
9. Bake 30 minutes, spraying every 3 to 4 minutes for the first 15 minutes of baking.
10. About 10 minutes before finished baking time, with a wire whip beat an egg white. Smooth over the hot loaves with a pastry brush and finish baking.
11. Remove immediately with a spatula, but very carefully.

**Tip:** If you have no rising cradles or unglazed quarry tiles, sprinkle cornmeal on the back of a large cookie sheet and arrange the loaves crosswise to rise. Cover and let rise. Put the pan of water in the oven with the brick in it and spray as explained in step 9. Also follow step 10.

**Tip:** When you keep the amount of yeast low, the dough rises more slowly and imparts greater elasticity, giving a good outside crust but wonderful soft bread inside.

## RISING CRADLES

The rising cradle mentioned in this series of recipes is of Lilian's own unique design. For each rising cradle cut two blocks of hardwood about ½" thick and 4½" square. Through each block bore two holes, 5/8" in diameter, near adjacent corners of the block.

Cut a piece of denim (or other heavy fabric) 18" long and 12" wide. Finish the 12" sides with a narrow hem to prevent fraying through repeated washings. Sew a 1" hem along the two 18" sides and thread a 5/8" dowel, 18" long, through each of these. Insert the ends of the dowels into the holes bored through the hardwood blocks. (The dowels should not be permanently attached; their easy removal allows for convenience in storage and for washing denim as needed.) The cradle hangs free and holds the loaves in shape while they are rising, giving a better shape to the finished loaves.

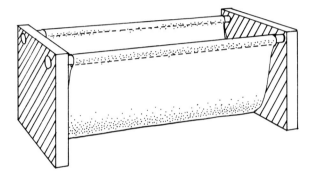

## UNGLAZED QUARRY TILES

Unglazed quarry tiles 6" x 6" x 5/8" can be purchased at a brickyard or a tile dealer. These are made of clay and are rather heavy. An ordinary oven usually requires six tiles, which are placed, close together and smooth side up, directly on the oven rack (for crusty baking) but do not completely cover the rack, leaving "breathing" space around the perimeter. This is mandatory for successful baking. The tiles need to be tempered through several bakings before the bread will no longer stick; therefore sprinkle cornmeal on the tiles to prevent sticking until they are well seasoned. Scrub the tiles after baking.

A set of six tiles and two rising cradles can be mail-ordered from Lilian DeLong (at the address given in our "Cook's Corner" under Lilian's Basic Specialty Bread Dough) for $19.50, which includes shipping costs.

# Italian Bread Sticks

(See photograph on page 36)

*Yield: The whole recipe makes 36 big bread sticks*

### Cook's Corner

*While making French Bread, why not make 1 loaf and use the other half of the dough to make 18 bread sticks?*

Use Lilian's Basic Specialty Bread Dough and proceed as follows:
1. Cut pieces a little bigger than a walnut.
2. Using only a light dusting of flour on the counter, roll each rope, with the palms of the hands, about the diameter of a pencil, 10" to 12" long.
3. Lay them crosswise on large greased cookie sheets (or sprinkle with cornmeal), allowing rising space between.
4. Brush with egg white or yolk, beaten with a wire whip.
5. Sprinkle with sesame or poppy seeds. Or season with garlic or minced onions, or dried Parmesan cheese, or paprika, or whatever you wish.
6. Let rise 20 to 30 minutes.
7. Bake 30 minutes at 325° F., or until a rich golden brown.
8. Take pan from oven and remove bread sticks with a spatula to cool on wire rack.
9. Keep in the air for crispness unless you live in a humid climate. You can re-crisp them by placing them on a cookie sheet in a 350° F. oven for a few minutes.

*"There is nothing wrong with mistakes, but don't respond to encores."*
Anonymous

# Pocket Bread (Pita Bread or Bible Bread)

(See photograph on page 36)

*Yield: 16 pockets*

Use Lilian's Basic Specialty Bread Dough and proceed as follows:

1. Cut into 16 portions about the size of a tennis ball. If you desire larger pockets, cut off larger pieces.
2. Cover with a towel or plastic wrap, as you work, to prevent dough from drying out. Roll each portion into a smooth ball.
3. With a rolling pin roll to 1/16″ thickness. Roll in one direction first, then in the other to keep the dough a round circle *without creases.* (Creases prevent the dough from forming a pocket.) If it is too thin or too thick it will not pocket well. A little practice will make it just right.
4. Preheat oven with tiles in place to 450° F. This high temperature will warp a cookie sheet, so tiles are recommended. Be sure the oven rack with tiles is on the bottom position.
5. As circles of dough are rolled, line them up to one side on the counter and let them rise. By the time the last is rolled, the first will be ready for baking. Bake only 4 at a time.
6. Bake at 450° F. for 2 to 3 minutes. They will be big puffs.
7. Turn over the puffs with a pancake turner. Brown both sides only slightly (2 to 3 minutes). Of course, turning over collapses the puffs a little bit.
8. Remove from oven with a spatula and cool on wire racks. Don't slit them until you are ready to use them. These can be stacked up and wrapped in plastic wrap for future use. Without any storage precautions, they will remain nice to eat for a couple of days or so; wrapped in plastic, they can also be frozen for future use.

**Tip:** Use part white flour and part whole wheat flour for a delicious pocket.

**Tip:** Take them on camping trips. Split the pocket at the top and the hollow opens up again. Or you can cut the circle in half and the hollow opens up for a pocket sandwich. These are delicious filled as you wish, like a taco, for example. Make a complete meal with refried beans, grated cheese, shredded lettuce; or use chopped dates or raisins with grated carrots; or fill with scrambled eggs—anything your imagination suggests. Enjoy!

*QUICK & EASY*

# Soft Pretzels

(See photograph on page 36)

*Yield: 24 pretzels*

The Basic Specialty Bread Dough needn't rise first when shaped for soft pretzels.

1. Cut dough into 24 pieces.
2. With very little flour on the board, roll each piece into a 14″ to 16″ long rope, about ½″ in diameter, moving palms of hands up and down the rope to keep it an even thickness.
3. Twist into pretzel shape by making a loop in the rope, forming a circle at the top. Twist ends around each other again.
4. Lift up the ends and lay them across the top of the loop; this makes a great pretzel shape. Place carefully on greased baking sheet. Use the back of the cookie sheet if you want them crusty.

1        2        3

5. Beat an egg white with wire whip and brush onto pretzel.
6. Sprinkle with coarse salt (rock salt may be ground in blender to desired coarseness). Or use other seasoning salt or dried cheese or sesame or poppy seed, as desired.

7. Bake about 15 minutes at 400° F., or until a rich golden brown.

**Tip:** For hard, skinny pretzels, like the commercial packaged ones, roll the ropes very skinny; form, and bake at a lower temperature and brush or spray with water during baking to develop crispness.

# Bagels

*Yield: 20 bagels*

Lilian's Basic Specialty Bread Dough can be enriched if you wish by adding 2 eggs and 3 tbsps vegetable oil. Then add a little more flour, as needed.

1. Cut dough into 20 pieces, and form into balls.
2. On countertop, lightly dusted with flour, with palms of hands roll each ball into strips about 6″ long and ¾″ thick.
3. Moisten ends with water and seal them together *well*, pinching ends together so they will adhere during boiling, making circles like doughnuts instead of separating and becoming horseshoes.
4. Let circles rise 15 to 20 minutes on countertop.
5. Dissolve 2 tbsps sugar into 2 quarts of water in a large saucepan and bring to a boil.
6. With spatula, lift bagels one at a time into the boiling water, boiling only 3 or 4 at a time to prevent crowding in the pan. (They expand a lot.)
7. Turn bagels over as they rise to the top and boil for 3 minutes, or as much as 6 minutes.
8. Remove from water with a slotted spoon and place on greased baking sheet.
9. Brush with mixture of 2 egg yolks and 2 tbsps water.
10. Bake plain, or season as desired with minced onion or Parmesan cheese or Lemon 'n Herb. Bake on cookie sheets 20 to 23 minutes at 425° F.
11. Remove from oven and cool on wire racks.

*QUICK & EASY*
# Pizza Crust

*Yield: 2 large cookie-sheet size or 3 round pizzas*

Use Lilian's Basic Specialty Bread Dough and divide into 2 or 3 pieces, as needed.
1. Roll each piece into a circle on a pastry cloth, the size of the pan plus 1 inch.
2. Grease pans or sprinkle with cornmeal.
3. Place dough circles on pans and, with fingers, form a lip all around the edge of the circles.
4. Let rise 10 to 20 minutes. For doughy crust, let it rise 30 minutes. Or no rise at all produces a crisp crust.
5. Bake 10 minutes at 425° F. to 450° F. Top crust as desired and return it to the oven for an additional 10 minutes of baking. (For a softer crust, bake 5 minutes initially.) Serve piping hot.

**Tip:** These crusts can be baked and frozen, then brought out of the freezer and topped with favorite fillings and baked 10 minutes.

# Hot Dog and Hamburger Buns

Use Lilian's Basic Specialty Dough recipe for making a different kind of bun. This has a crunchy crust instead of soft, and the inside is soft and elastic. Form the buns as described in the basic Hot Dog and Hamburger Buns recipe on page 13. Place on the greased backs of cookie sheets, leaving room for rising. Let buns rise until almost double in bulk. Brush tops with beaten egg, if desired. Bake about 20 minutes at 375° F. to 400° F. or until golden brown. Remove from oven and cool on wire racks.

# Louise's Raised Doughnuts

(See photograph on page 34)

*Yield: 2 to 3 dozen (plus "holes," depending on size)*

### Cook's Corner

*This recipe was handed down from Louise's mother-in-law, who received it from her mother-in-law—a Squire family old favorite.*

*You will enjoy making these more if you have a helper to keep the glazing in process while doughnuts are frying.*

*For superior raised doughnuts, use a "spudnut" cutter which has a proportionally smaller hole in the middle. These are hard to find. Try a wholesale restaurant supply house. If one is not available, use a vegetable can and the detachable hole in a doughnut cutter, or a small screw-on salt shaker top will do.*

½ cup mashed potatoes
½ cup warm potato water
1 cup milk
¼ cup warm water (115° F.)
1 tbsp active dry yeast
¼ cup margarine or butter
2 eggs, well beaten
½ cup sugar
½ tsp salt
½ tsp nutmeg
about 4 cups all-purpose flour

1. If leftover mashed potatoes and leftover potato water are not available, cook a potato in a small saucepan. Mash the potato right in the cooking water to make a total of 1 cup. If using leftover mashed potatoes, potato water is not necessary.
2. In a small saucepan, scald milk and add butter to melt as milk cools.
3. In a small bowl, set yeast to dissolve in ¼ cup warm water.
4. In a large mixer bowl, combine milk mixture, yeast, sugar, beaten eggs, salt, nutmeg, and 2 cups of flour. Beat until smooth. Add remaining flour. This will be a very soft, sticky dough.
5. Let rise, then stir down.
6. Let rise a second time.
7. Stir down and turn out on *generously* floured surface, kneading just enough to roll the dough. For light raised doughnuts, keep dough very soft, not stiff at all.
8. Roll the dough into a large circle about 5/8″ thick. Cut with "spudnut" cutter, then spread them out on floured surface to allow rising room.
9. Let rise until about double in bulk, about 20 minutes.
10. Deep fry at 350° F. to 375° F. until golden brown on one side. With a fork, turn them over.
11. Remove doughnuts when golden to drain on paper towel on wire racks.
12. While raised doughnuts are still very warm, quickly drop them, one at a time, into bowl of glaze, coating well, then let excess drip back into the bowl. Place glazed doughnuts on paper towel on rack so glaze can set up. Fry and glaze the holes, too.

## BASIC GLAZE:

(Make this while raised doughnuts are rising, before frying.)
1 cup *hot* water
2 1-pound boxes of powdered sugar
1 tsp vanilla
pinch of salt

Beat all ingredients together in deep mixing bowl large enough to accommodate the big doughnuts, one at a time.

Try different glazes as desired: maple glaze (see under LaVerne's Maple Bars), chocolate (by adding 2 tbsps cocoa), or orange (using basic glaze recipe, squeeze orange and use juice for part of hot water; grate the rind and add to glaze).

**Tip:** For storing, do not stack raised doughnuts. And do not cover with plastic wrap or foil, which causes sweating. Use a cardboard box or tray and turn doughnuts on the side, lining them up as in bakery counters. Don't crowd them. Cover with a towel.

**Tip:** Freeze some. When they are needed, remove from the freezer and microwave them. Microwave only as many as are needed for immediate consumption.

# LaVerne's Maple Bars

*Yield: About 4 dozen*

## Cook's Corner

*This recipe is a favorite with the Darrington family. Whether it be at a ward bazaar or fund-raiser or even at the county fair, LaVerne is in demand with her Maple Bars. Made on the spot for immediate sale and enjoyment, the bars have a most inviting aroma. Although she makes them by the hundreds, I have cut the recipe down to family size. Even then, you'll want to share with the neighbors.*

2 cups warm water (115° F.)
1 tbsp active dry yeast
¼ tsp sugar
2 eggs, beaten
⅓ cup powdered milk
¼ cup vegetable oil
2 tsps salt
¼ cup sugar
about 5 to 6 cups all-purpose flour

1.  In large mixer bowl, sprinkle yeast and ¼ tsp sugar in warm water to dissolve.
2.  Beat eggs well in small mixer bowl.
3.  To the dissolved yeast mixture add beaten eggs, powdered milk, oil, salt, and sugar with 3 cups flour and beat until smooth.
4.  Add 2 cups more flour gradually. This should be a sticky dough, not stiff enough to knead.
5.  Let rise in bowl. Stir down.
6.  Let rise again. Stir down.
7.  Turn out onto *generously* floured board or pastry cloth and mix in more flour only until it can be rolled out.
8.  With pizza cutter, cut strips about 2″ x 3½″. Separate and spread out the dough strips on floured surface so they will not stick together.
9.  Let rise about 20 minutes then start deep frying in oil heated to about 350° F. to 375° F.
10. Turn over the bars when the first side is golden. Cook both sides to golden.
11. When bars are cooked, remove carefully with fork or tongs and place on paper towels on racks to drain.
12. When partially cool, ice with maple glaze.

## MAPLE GLAZE:

1 ½ cups powdered sugar
1 tsp maple flavoring

Use *hot* water to make frosting a medium consistency. If the glaze is too soft it will just run off. Start with 3 tbsps and increase water as needed.

**Tip:** Do not cover Maple Bars with plastic wrap or foil. This causes sweating and the glaze will run. Do not stack them. Stand them up on sides, uncrowded, in a tray or cookie sheet with sides. Cover with a towel.

*"Happiness adds and multiplies as we divide it with others."*
Anonymous

# Quick Breads, Waffles, and Hotcakes

(For an explanation of any unfamiliar ingredients listed in these recipes, see the discussion on Ingredients in the last section of this book.)

## Crackers

(See photograph on page 45)

*Yield: 2 to 3 dozen 1½-inch-square crackers*

1 cup all-purpose flour
½ tsp salt
½ tsp baking powder
2 tbsps butter or margarine
1 egg
¼ cup milk

1. Into a medium-sized mixing bowl, sift together flour, salt, and soda.
2. With pastry blender, cut butter into dry ingredients as for pie crust.
3. Beat egg and add milk, then add to flour mixture. Stir with a fork until blended, then turn out onto floured surface and knead a few minutes until a smooth ball is formed, adding a little flour only as necessary to prevent sticking.
4. With rolling pin, roll out to an oblong about 5″ x 11″ and transfer to the greased back of a large cookie sheet. Brace the cookie sheet to the back of the counter top and roll as thin as possible. Keep edges a little thicker to prevent burning.
5. Sprinkle with coarse salt or favorite seasoning salt. (I like Lemon 'n Herb.)
6. Bake on top rack in preheated oven at 375° F. to 400° F. for 10 to 12 minutes until lightly brown.
7. Remove from oven and immediately cut into squares with pizza cutter. If necessary, spread out crackers and return to oven for a few minutes longer for crispness. Lower oven heat to 350° F.

**Tip:** Double recipe for larger quantity and use 2 cookie sheets.

### VARIATIONS:

1. *Soda Crackers:* Substitute buttermilk for milk and baking soda for baking powder; proceed as above.
2. *Rye Wafers* (see photograph on page 45): Substitute rye flour for all-purpose flour. Use baking powder and milk. Add 1 or 2 teaspoons caraway seeds.

## Graham Crackers

(See photograph on page 45)

*Yield: 4 dozen 1½″ to 2″ crackers*

2 cups whole wheat flour
2 tsps baking powder
¼ tsp salt
⅓ cup brown sugar
⅓ cup margarine or butter
½ cup milk

1. Sift together flour, baking powder, salt, and brown sugar into a small mixing bowl.
2. With pastry blender, cut in butter.
3. Add milk and blend. Turn out onto floured surface and knead into a ball.
4. Roll dough into an oblong about 5″ x 11″. Transfer this oblong to the greased back of a cookie sheet. Roll out thin to edges of cookie sheet, keeping edges slightly thicker to prevent burning.
5. Bake 8 to 10 minutes at 375° F. to 400° F. or until lightly brown.

6.  Remove from oven and with a pizza cutter immediately cut into squares.
7.  Separate the squares a bit and return to the oven a few minutes longer for a crisper cracker.

## Cheese Balls

*Yield: 2 dozen*

### Cook's Corner

*These balls are perfect as a luncheon salad accompaniment.*

5-oz. jar of sharp cheese
¼ cup butter
1 cup sifted flour

1.  In a medium-sized mixing bowl, cream the cheese and butter.
2.  Add flour and mix well with hands.
3.  Chill dough for 2 hours if possible. However, if time is limited, chilling is not imperative. Make 1″ balls and place on lightly greased cookie sheet.
4.  Bake at 375° F. for about 15 minutes. Serve piping hot or cold.

If larger quantity is desired, double the recipe.

## Whole Wheat Apricot Bread

*Yield: 2 medium loaves*

¾ cup water
½ cup dried apricots, snipped
½ cup raisins
½ cup walnuts
1½ cups whole wheat flour
½ cup brown sugar, packed
¼ cup granulated sugar
1 tsp baking powder
½ tsp baking soda
½ tsp salt
¼ cup margarine or butter
2 eggs, slightly beaten
1 tsp vanilla

1.  In a medium-sized saucepan, combine water, snipped apricots, and raisins and bring to a boil (Cut apricots with kitchen scissors.) Chop walnuts.
2.  Into a large mixing bowl sift the flour, sugars, baking powder, soda, and salt.
3.  Remove fruit mixture from burner. Add margarine and let it melt as fruit cools.
4.  With wire whip, beat the eggs in a medium-sized mixing bowl.
5.  Add fruit mixture, eggs, and vanilla to dry ingredients in bowl and stir well.
6.  Fold in walnuts.
7.  Pour into 2 greased and floured pans 7½″ x 3½″ or use 3 cans (16-oz. vegetable size).
8.  Bake 40 to 45 minutes at 350° F. or until inserted toothpick comes out clean. Remove from oven, let stand 5 minutes, and turn out on wire rack to cool.

## Chewy-Top Banana Bread

*Yield: 1 large loaf*

1 cup 100% Bran cereal
¾ cup walnuts
2 tbsps brown sugar
1 tbsp butter, melted
½ cup butter or margarine
1 cup granulated sugar
1 tsp vanilla
1 egg
2 medium-sized ripe bananas (about 1 cup)
2 cups sifted all-purpose flour
2 tsps baking powder
½ tsp baking soda
¼ tsp salt
½ cup buttermilk

1.  Melt butter in a small saucepan.
2.  With a rolling pin, crush the cereal to crumbs. Chop walnuts.
3.  In a small bowl combine crumbs, chopped nuts, brown sugar and melted butter.
4.  Set aside ½ cup of the crumb mixture in a cup.

*Facing page:* Sourdough White Bread (p. 76); 100% Whole Wheat Sourdough Bread (p. 78); Sourdough Buns (p. 79)

5. In the large bowl of mixer, cream until fluffy ½ cup butter and granulated sugar. Add vanilla.
6. Add egg and bananas. Beat until smooth.
7. Sift together the flour, baking powder, soda, and salt twice.
8. Add buttermilk and sifted dry ingredients; mix well.
9. Fold in leftover crumb mixture.
10. Pour into 2 greased and floured pans 7½" x 3½".
11. Sprinkle reserved crumb mixture on top.
12. Bake 55 to 60 minutes at 350° F. or until inserted toothpick comes out clean.
13. Cool 10 minutes in pan.
14. Remove from pan and cool on wire rack.

## VARIATION:

Other prepared cereals, such as Rice Krispies or Special K, can also be used.

# Apple Bread

*Yield: 1 large loaf*

½ cup chopped nuts
1 to 1 ½ cups unpeeled grated raw apple
2 cups all-purpose flour
1 tsp baking powder
½ tsp baking soda
1 tsp cinnamon
½ cup butter or margarine
¾ cup sugar
2 eggs
1 tsp vanilla

**Topping:**
2 tbsps sugar
¼ cup finely chopped nuts
½ tsp cinnamon
1 tsp water

1. Place finely chopped nuts in a separate cup for topping.
2. Mix topping by combining all the topping ingredients in the cup with nuts.
3. In a medium-sized bowl, grate unpeeled apple. The variable amount depends on the size of the

apple; a little more or less won't matter. Set aside.
4. Sift together twice the flour, baking powder, soda, and cinnamon. Set aside.
5. Cream butter, sugar, and eggs until fluffy and add vanilla.
6. Add sifted dry ingredients and grated apples; blend well.
7. Pour batter into greased and floured loaf pan 8½" x 4½".
8. Sprinkle topping over top of batter and bake 45 to 50 minutes at 325° F. to 350° F. or until a toothpick inserted in the baked bread comes out clean.
9. Remove from oven, let stand in pan 5 to 10 minutes, then carefully turn out onto wire rack to cool.

# Banana Bread

(See photograph on page 46)

*Yield: 1 loaf*

### Cook's Corner
*This is a good way to use those overripe bananas.*

2 ¼ cups sifted all-purpose flour
¼ tsp salt
1 tsp nutmeg
2 eggs
2 large bananas
¼ cup margarine (½ cube)
½ cup granulated sugar
½ cup brown sugar
1 tsp soda
3 tbsps buttermilk
1 cup nuts, chopped

1. Sift the flour, salt, and nutmeg together twice. Set aside.
2. Separate eggs; place whites in small mixer bowl and yolks in large mixer bowl. Beat whites until stiff. Set aside.
3. To egg yolks in large bowl add bananas, margarine, and sugars. Cream until smooth and fluffy.

*Facing page:* Breads for celiacs: Gluten-Free Bread with Yeast (p. 82), and Low-Gluten Wheat-Free Bread (Non-Yeast) (p. 84)

4. Dissolve soda in buttermilk and add to creamed mixture, together with sifted dry ingredients. Mix well.
5. Fold in egg whites and nuts.
6. Pour batter into greased and floured loaf pan 8½" x 4½".
7. Bake at 350° F. to 375° F. for 45 to 50 minutes or until inserted toothpick comes out clean.
8. Remove from oven. Let stand 5 to 10 minutes in pan, then turn out onto wire rack to cool.

**Tip:** This is also delicious with 2 cups whole wheat flour substituted for the all-purpose flour.

# Zucchini Bread

*Yield: 2 loaves*

### Cook's Corner

*This is a good way to use up that oversized zucchini.*

2 cups peeled and grated zucchini
3 cups all-purpose flour
1 tsp salt
¼ tsp baking powder
1 tsp soda
¾ tsp nutmeg
3 tsps cinnamon
3 eggs
2 cups sugar
1 cup vegetable oil
3 tsps vanilla
1 cup nuts, chopped

1. Peel and grate zucchini. Set aside.
2. Sift together flour, salt, baking powder, soda, and spices. Set aside.
3. In large mixer bowl, beat eggs thoroughly.
4. Add oil, sugar, vanilla, zucchini, and sifted dry ingredients. Mix well.
5. Fold in nuts.
6. Pour into greased and floured 8½" x 4½" loaf pans and bake 1 hour at 325° F. to 350° F.
7. Remove from oven when inserted toothpick comes out clean. Let stand in pan 5 minutes, then turn out onto wire rack to cool.

**Tip:** Do not store in plastic; wrap in a clean dish towel so it will not become wet. This bread also freezes well. Wrap in plastic or foil for freezing. Remove from plastic when partially thawed to prevent sweating.

# Myrtle's Pumpkin Bread

(See photograph on page 46)

*Yield: See second Tip below*

3 ½ cups all-purpose flour
  (spooned but unsifted)
1 ¾ cups sugar
1 ½ tsps baking soda
1 ½ tsps baking powder
1 tsp salt
1 tsp cinnamon
1 tsp nutmeg
½ tsp cloves
4 eggs
¾ cup water
7/8 cup oil
2 tsps vanilla
2 cups pumpkin (1-lb. can)
½ cup walnuts, chopped

1. Sift together 3 times the flour, sugar, baking soda, baking powder, salt, cinnamon, nutmeg, and cloves. The third time, sift it right into a large mixer bowl.
2. In the small mixer bowl, beat the eggs until thick and fluffy.
3. To the dry ingredients add the eggs, water, oil, vanilla, and pumpkin; beat well.
4. Fold in nuts.
5. Pour batter into greased and floured loaf pans.
6. Bake in preheated oven 50 to 60 minutes at 350° F. to 375° F. or until an inserted toothpick comes out smooth.
7. Remove from oven and let stand in pans for 5 minutes before turning out onto wire racks to cool.

**Tip:** A finer texture is achieved with the mixer than mixing by hand.

**Tip:** This recipe makes 8 very small loaves baked in pans 4½″ x 2½″ or 4 medium-sized loaves in pans 7½″ x 3½″, or 2 large loaves in pans 8½″ x 4½″. Adjust baking time according to pan sizes, less time for the smaller pans.

**Tip:** This bread freezes well. Wrap tightly in plastic wrap.

When pumpkin bread is not eaten within a day after baking, you may find the top becomes wet if stored in a plastic bag. If so, wrap it in a towel and it will remain moist for several days.

## VARIATION:

Try different kinds of nuts. Almonds and peanuts are cheaper than walnuts and give a totally different flavor.

# Pumpkin Muffins

(See photograph on page 46)

*Yield: 1 dozen muffins*

1 ½ cups all-purpose flour
⅓ cup sugar
1 ½ tsps baking powder
½ tsp salt
½ tsp cinnamon
½ tsp nutmeg
¼ cup (half a cube) butter or margarine
1 egg
½ cup milk
½ cup cooked and mashed or canned pumpkin

**Topping:**

2 tsps sugar
¼ tsp cinnamon
¼ cup almonds, ground in blender (optional)
½ cup raisins (optional)
½ cup chocolate chips (optional)

1. Into mixing bowl, sift together twice flour, sugar, baking powder, salt, and spices.
2. With pastry blender, cut margarine into flour mixture until crumbly.
3. Beat egg and add to crumbs with milk and pumpkin. Blend well.

4. Spoon batter into muffin tins (1 dozen).
5. Combine 2 tsp sugar, cinnamon, and ground almonds, sprinkle on top of each muffin.
6. Bake about 20 minutes at 375° F. to 400° F.

**Tip:** The addition of raisins and/or chocolate chips makes a delicious cupcake.

# Whole Wheat Muffins

*Yield: 1 dozen*

2 cups sifted whole wheat flour
½ tsp salt
3 tsps baking powder
2 eggs
1 cup milk
3 tbsps raw or brown sugar
2 tbsps melted butter or vegetable oil

1. Sift together twice the flour, salt, and baking powder.
2. In the small mixer bowl, beat eggs; add milk, sugar, and oil.
3. Stir in dry ingredients only until flour mixture is absorbed. Do not beat.
4. Spoon into greased muffin tins and bake 20 to 30 minutes at 375° F. to 400° F.

**Tip:** For a richer muffin, increase sugar to ⅓ cup and oil to ¼ cup.

## VARIATIONS:

1. Blueberry muffins: Add ¾ cup fresh or frozen blueberries, or well-drained canned berries.
2. Date or nut muffins: Add ½ cup dates or nuts.
3. Old-fashioned cornmeal muffins: Substitute 1 cup cornmeal for 1 cup whole wheat flour.

—From Vernice G. Rosenvall, Mabel H. Miller, and Dora D. Flack, *Wheat for Man: Why and How*, 3rd ed. (Salt Lake City: Bookcraft, 1975), p. 47.

# Karla's Indian Bread

*Yield: 8 pieces*

### Cook's Corner

*Karla's family enjoys this for a special, quick hot-bread treat with dinner.*

2 cups all-purpose flour
½ tsp salt
2 tsps baking powder
½ cup water

1. Sift together dry ingredients into medium-sized mixing bowl.
2. Add water and knead well into a ball. Turn out on well-floured surface.
3. Roll out in a circle, as thin as possible.
4. With pizza cutter, cut into 8 pieces.
5. Fry in oil until golden on one side. Turn over and fry the other side. Serve piping hot, plain, or with butter and honey.

Multiply the measurements to suit your family's size and appetite.

# Baking Powder Biscuits (Supreme)

*Yield: 16 medium-sized biscuits*

2 cups flour, unsifted
½ tsp salt
3 tsps baking powder
½ tsp cream of tartar
2 tsps sugar
½ cup shortening
1 cup milk

1. Sift together flour, salt, baking powder, cream of tartar, and sugar.
2. Cut in shortening with pastry blender until mixture resembles coarse crumbs.
3. Add milk all at once and stir with fork lightly just until blended and turn out onto generously floured breadboard.

4. Pat or roll dough very lightly to ½-inch thickness. Sprinkle top of dough with a bit of flour.
5. Cut with biscuit cutter or cut in diamond shapes with pizza cutter.
6. Bake on ungreased cookie sheet 10 to 12 minutes at 425° F. to 450° F. or until golden brown. Serve piping hot.

# Buttermilk Biscuits

*Yield: 16 medium-sized biscuits*

2 cups flour, unsifted
½ tsp salt
½ tsp cream of tartar
2 tsps sugar
½ cup shortening
1 tsp soda, dissolved in
1 cup buttermilk

Prepare according to instructions for Baking Powder Biscuits.

# Corn Bread

*Yield: 9 large squares*

⅓ cup butter
1 cup yellow cornmeal
1 cup all-purpose flour
½ tsp salt
½ cup sugar
2 eggs, beaten
½ tsp soda
1 cup buttermilk (or ½ cup plain yogurt and ½ cup water)

1. Melt butter in small saucepan.
2. Sift cornmeal, flour, and salt twice. Set aside.
3. Remove melted butter from heat and add sugar.
4. In medium-sized bowl beat eggs very well and add melted butter and sugar, beating well.
5. Dissolve soda in buttermilk and add with sifted dry ingredients to egg mixture. Mix thoroughly.

6. Pour into greased 8″ x 8″ pan.
7. Bake about 30 minutes at 375° F. to 400° F.
8. Remove from oven. Cut in squares and serve piping hot.

**Tip:** In place of buttermilk, add milk to 2 tbsps vinegar or lemon juice to make a full cup.

**Tip:** Even leftover corn bread is delicious when squares are cut in half, buttered, and toasted under the broiler, or it can be heated and served with syrup or jam and enjoyed like pancakes or French toast.

# Eve's Potato-Cornmeal Triangles

*Yield: 12 triangles*

⅔ cup *hot* tap water
⅔ cup instant mashed potato flakes
½ cup shortening or margarine
1 egg
1¼ cups sifted all-purpose flour
2 tbsps sugar
3 tsps baking powder
½ tsp salt
½ cup cornmeal
⅓ cup milk

1. Pour hot water into a medium-sized saucepan.
2. With a wire whip, stir potato flakes into hot water until mixture is absorbed.
3. Blend in shortening.
4. Beat egg and stir in.
5. Sift together flour, sugar, baking powder, salt, and cornmeal.
6. Add milk and sifted dry ingredients to potato mixture and blend.
7. Turn dough onto well-floured surface and knead 3 or 4 times.
8. Roll into 9-inch circle. With pizza cutter, cut into 12 triangles. Place on slightly greased baking sheet about 2 inches apart.
9. Bake at 400° F. for 20 minutes.
10. Remove from oven and serve piping hot.

**Tip:** Leftover triangles can be slit and reheated under the broiler. Butter first, if desired.

# Quick Mix

8 cups all-purpose flour
¼ cup baking powder, plus 2 tsps
4 tsps salt
¼ cup sugar
2 cups shortening

1. Sift together twice into large bowl the flour, baking powder, salt and sugar.
2. With pastry blender, cut in shortening.
3. Store in covered jar in refrigerator and mix as needed.

Quick Mix will keep for 1 to 2 months in the refrigerator. It can be used as desired for the following three recipes.

# Quick Mix Biscuits

*Yield: Approximately 8*

1 cup Quick Mix
about ¼ cup milk

1. Add milk to Quick Mix in a small bowl and mix lightly with hand.
2. Roll about 5/8″ thick on floured board.
3. Cut with round cookie cutter. Or for speed, cut with sharp knife into diamond shapes.
4. Bake 12 to 15 minutes at 375° F. to 400° F. until lightly browned. Serve piping hot.

# Quick Mix Hotcakes

*Yield: Approximately 8*

1 egg, beaten
1 tbsp sugar
1 cup milk
1⅓ cups Quick Mix

1. Beat egg in small mixer bowl.
2. Add sugar and milk; spoon in Quick Mix. Blend.
3. Bake on hot griddle.

**Tip:** This is ideal for camping trips. For greater convenience, add 2 cups powdered milk to basic Quick Mix ingredients above, then use only water instead of milk.

# Quick Mix Meat Pie

*Serves 6*

### Cook's Corner

*I love to cook a roast for the family and make brown gravy. I use the leftover roast and gravy in the next day or two to make stew or meat pie. Even company is generous with raves. "This meat pie is fit for a king," they say. And yet it is so simple.*

2 cups cubed leftover roast, or 1 can of meat
3 medium-sized potatoes, diced
3 carrots, diced or sliced
1 medium-sized onion, diced
1 stalk celery, diced
any leftover vegetables, such as corn, green beans, or peas
salt and pepper to taste
1 tsp ground sage

1. Peel and prepare fresh vegetables and place in medium-sized saucepan. Add water but don't quite cover vegetables. Cook until almost tender.
2. Add vegetable leftovers, meat, and seasonings.
3. Place in large greased 3-qt. casserole dish.
4. Top with pie crust and bake 25 to 30 minutes at 375° F. to 400° F. Serve piping hot with hot brown gravy.

### PIE CRUST FOR MEAT PIE:
3 cups Quick Mix
¾ cup milk

1. With fork, mix together the Quick Mix and milk and turn out onto well-floured surface. Roll into a large circle or oval to fit 3-quart casserole dish. Slash 4 or 5 slits for steam to escape.

2. Cover vegetable-meat mixture with dough, crimp around the edges and bake as above.

**Tip:** If leftover brown gravy is not available, use commercial gravy mix.

**Tip:** If your family is small, use this for two or more meals. Put in individual baking dishes or 1½-qt. baking dishes. Divide vegetables into greased baking dishes. Roll dough to fit each. Cover with plastic wrap or foil and freeze. About 24 hours before baking, remove from freezer and thaw in the refrigerator.

## VARIATIONS:

1. Hamburger can be browned and used in place of leftover roast.
2. Roll dough out and use widemouthed jar lid to cut rounds of dough. Line buttered muffin tins with dough. Add vegetables. For last 5 minutes of baking time, sprinkle grated cheese on top and return to oven to finish baking.

If you wish to freeze some of these, bake only a few minutes, then cool, wrap and freeze. Thaw only the number needed for baking, putting cheese on the tops.
3. Use leftover chicken or turkey instead of beef and proceed as above.

# Oat Pancakes

*Yield: About 8, depending on size*

½ cup whole wheat flour
1½ tsps baking powder
pinch of salt
1 tbsp sugar
2 eggs, separated
1 cup milk
3 tbsps vegetable oil
1 cup quick oats

1. Sift the flour, baking powder, salt, and sugar together twice.
2. Beat egg whites in small mixing bowl. Set aside.
3. In large mixing bowl, beat egg yolks, milk, oil, and oats.

4. Add dry ingredients and lightly blend.
5. Fold in beaten egg whites.
6. Bake on hot griddle until brown on one side. Turn carefully and brown the other side.

Serve with apple sauce or your favorite jam or butter and maple syrup.

# Geraldine's R & R Pancakes

*Yield: 8 to 10, depending on size*

## Cook's Corner

*This recipe is excellent for people who cannot tolerate wheat. However, it's equally delicious and nutritious for anyone.*

¾ cup rye flour
¾ cup rice flour
1 tbsp baking powder
½ tsp salt
2 tbsps sugar or honey
2 eggs, separated
3 tbsps vegetable oil
1 ½ cups milk

1. Sift together rye and rice flours with baking powder, salt, and sugar.
2. Separate eggs and beat whites until stiff. Set aside.
3. Beat egg yolks in small mixer bowl.
4. Add oil, sweetener, and milk.
5. Add sifted dry ingredients and blend.
6. Fold in beaten egg whites.
7. Bake on griddle until bubbles form and bottom is nicely browned. Turn over to brown other side.
8. Serve piping hot with butter, syrup, or jam. Or serve with fresh strawberries and whipped cream for a festive dessert.

# Waffles

## (Extremely light)

*Yield: 3 or 4*

## Cook's Corner

*For Sunday night suppers, the Bankhead family's favorite is Mary's Strawberry Sundae Waffles. Mary purees fresh strawberries in the blender until they form a thick topping and sweetens them slightly. Over these wheat waffles she pours a little maple syrup; then a scoop of vanilla ice cream, in the middle of the waffle, is topped with the strawberry puree. For extra eye appeal, a few whole berries are added. What a delectable dish! Try it.*

1 cup sifted whole wheat flour
3 tsps baking powder
½ tsp salt
3 tsps brown sugar
2 eggs, separated
¼ cup vegetable oil
1 ¼ cups milk

1. Sift the flour, baking powder, salt, and sugar together three times.
2. Separate eggs and beat the whites in the small mixer bowl. Set aside.
3. Beat egg yolks in medium-sized bowl and add oil, milk, and sifted dry ingredients. Beat for two minutes. Batter will be very thin.
4. Fold in egg whites.
5. Bake in preheated waffle iron.

Serve with apple sauce, table cream, or your favorite syrup.

## VARIATION:

Add 1 tsp soda and substitute buttermilk for milk.

—From Vernice G. Rosenvall, Mabel H. Miller, and Dora D. Flack, *Wheat for Man: Why and How*, 3rd ed. (Salt Lake City: Bookcraft, 1975), p. 49.

# Deluxe Hotcakes

*Yield: 8 to 10, depending on size*

1 ½ cups sifted whole wheat flour
1 tbsp baking powder
¾ tsp salt
3 tbsps brown sugar
2 eggs, separated
1 ½ cups whole milk
3 tbsps vegetable oil

1.  Sift the flour, baking powder, salt, and sugar together twice. Set aside.
2.  Separate eggs. Put whites in the small mixer bowl and yolks in a medium-sized mixing bowl. Beat egg whites and set aside.
3.  Beat egg yolks, milk, and oil.
4.  Add sifted dry ingredients and blend.
5.  Fold in beaten egg whites.
6.  Bake on lightly greased hot griddle.

Serve with butter and syrup or with apple sauce.

—From Vernice G. Rosenvall, Mabel H. Miller, and Dora D. Flack, *Wheat for Man: Why and How*, 3rd ed. (Salt Lake City: Bookcraft, 1975), p. 49.

# Blender Pancakes

*Yield: 8*

## Cook's Corner

*Trust me. This really works!*

1 cup wheat kernels, washed
1 ¼ cups milk
1 egg
⅓ cup vegetable oil
1 tbsp baking powder
½ tsp salt
1 ½ tbsps sugar, if desired

1.  Wash wheat; drain off water and place in blender.

2.  Add milk and blend on highest speed 3 to 5 minutes.
3.  Add egg, oil, baking powder, salt, and sugar. Blend 1 to 2 minutes longer.
4.  Pour from blender onto hot griddle in puddles about 3 to 4 inches in diameter.
5.  Bake until bottom is nicely browned. Turn with spatula and brown the other side.

Serve with apple sauce, butter and syrup, or your favorite jam. These are chewy and filling and *soooo* good.

**Tip:** Leftover pancakes can be placed in sandwich bags and frozen, then dropped into the toaster for heating just before serving.

# Buttermilk Blender Pancakes

*Yield: 8*

1 cup wheat kernels, washed
1 ½ cups buttermilk
1 egg
⅓ cup vegetable oil
½ tsp salt
1 ½ tbsps sugar, if desired
1 tsp baking soda

Follow instructions for Blender Pancakes.

*"Economy makes happy homes and sound nations; instill it deep."*
Anonymous

# Hootenanny Hotcakes

*Yield: 8 to 10, depending on size of servings*

## Cook's Corner

*This can be served as a main dish with crisp bacon and a salad; or it becomes dessert when served with fruit or sweet topping. It's a great party dish for young people because a second pan can be whipped up quickly while the first panful is being enjoyed.*

1 cup all-purpose flour
½ tsp salt
½ cup butter or margarine
6 eggs, beaten
1 cup milk

1. Sift together flour and salt. Set aside.
2. Melt butter in 9″ x 12″ pan or 10″ x 13″ jelly roll pan.
3. Preheat oven to 400° F. to 425° F.
4. Beat eggs in small mixer bowl until thick and lemony. Do not underbeat.
5. Add milk and flour. Stir only until dry ingredients are blended.
6. Pour batter over butter in pan.
7. Immediately bake 20 to 25 minutes at 400° F. to 425° F.
8. When very lightly browned, remove from oven, cut into squares, and serve *immediately*. Quickly and lightly sprinkle with lemon juice and powdered sugar. Or serve like pancakes with syrup, jam, or jelly. Or top with sliced fresh fruit, such as strawberries, raspberries, or peaches.

**Tip:** If preparing for a small family, cut recipe in half and bake in 8″ x 8″ square pan.

# Mother's Doughnuts

*Yield: About 3 dozen*

## Cook's Corner

*Mother made doughnuts for special occasions, holidays, or visits of grandchildren who all remember her for this special delight. She was reared on a farm and insisted that lard was necessary for these doughnuts, for both mixing and frying. However, they are also successful with shortening and oil. She liked to wait until one of us daughters was available to assist with the frying while she mixed and cut. Her recipe was in the feel of her fingers until Bonnie, a granddaughter, helped her one day and reduced it to measurements so we all can make them, now that Mother is gone. We recall pleasant times in Mother's kitchen as we nibble.*

3 to 4 cups all-purpose flour
1 tsp salt
2 ½ tsps baking powder
1 tsp nutmeg
2 eggs
1 cup sugar
2 tbsps shortening
1 cup milk
oil for frying
½ cup granulated sugar for coating

1. Sift together 3 cups flour, salt, baking powder, and nutmeg. Set aside.
2. Beat eggs in medium-sized bowl.
3. To the eggs, add sugar and shortening and beat well.
4. Add milk with sifted dry ingredients and beat, adding up to 1 cup flour as needed to make a *soft* dough. The stiffer the dough, the heavier the finished doughnuts will be.
5. Turn out on generously floured surface, preferably a pastry cloth. Pat out dough or roll *very lightly* about ½ inch thick. Do not be heavy-handed with a rolling pin.
6. Cut with doughnut cutter. Bits of dough cut away can be remixed gently and re-rolled for more doughnuts.
7. Heat oil in deep fryer to 350° F. to 375° F. Test for the right heat by dropping in a "hole" to see how fast it browns. Fry one side, then turn

over with a fork. (A plastic fork is great.) When doughnuts are browned on both sides, remove and drain on paper towel.

8. Place ½ cup sugar in a small mixing bowl. Dip warm doughnuts in sugar and place on rack to cool.

**Tip:** For storing, never put these doughnuts in plastic. Mother always lined a large kettle with a clean dishtowel and carefully placed the doughnuts inside, covered them with the towel, then put the lid on. They keep well this way for several days. I thought I was being progressive when I stored them in plastic bags. Wrong. They sweat. So now I use Mother's tried-and-true storage method.

*"Do you love me
Or do you not?
You told me once
But I forgot."*

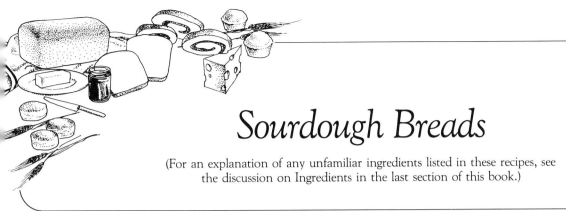

# Sourdough Breads

(For an explanation of any unfamiliar ingredients listed in these recipes, see
the discussion on Ingredients in the last section of this book.)

**B**reads need leavening (rising) agents, usually yeast.

In the nineteenth century, when pioneering expansion was extensive, bread was the staple of life, especially for the "Sourdoughs" of California and Alaska gold rushes. Yet in those days yeast was difficult to keep alive. Chuckwagon cooks developed their own leavening agent—sourdough starters. Sometimes those inventive cooks supplied the necessary warmth for their starters by taking them to bed to keep them alive. Sometimes a Sourdough carried his starter inside his shirt in cold weather to maintain its temperature. Thus it was always ready to be used in bread, muffins, rolls, and even pancakes.

That tangy sourdough flavor is a favorite with many today. Some bakeries have built their reputations on sourdough products. Yet you can make these products in your own kitchen.

The sourdough starter is the first requisite. George Mardikian, who built and operated Omar Khayyam's Restaurant in San Francisco, regarded sourdough as a necessity. He said, "If you don't have a starter, look in the telephone book and find any name ending with 'ian'. You'll know you've found an Armenian and he will share his starter with you."

Sourdough enthusiasts tell us that the older the starter, the better it is, and many of them have interesting histories. However, don't despair if you can't find one—our Sourdough Starter recipe will tell you how to make your own! With proper care and feeding, yours too will become strong. And if it gives out, you can always start a new one.

Tastes vary, of course. Children usually prefer the milder flavor, especially until they develop a heightened taste for sourdough.

Don't be afraid to play with this. It's a "live" product and has resilience. And it is rewarding to use.

Everything I have read on sourdough specifies the use of glass bowls *only* and wooden spoons. However, reflection on the lifestyle of the old sourdough cooks tells us that glass would have been far too fragile for their travel and working conditions. They often used metal pans coated with "enamel," or clay crockware coated with enamel. Taking a cue from this, I experimented with stainless-steel bowls and utensils, not ordinary metal. My results were the same as when I used a glass bowl and wooden spoon. In the recipes of this section I will retain the caution to use glass bowls and wooden spoons, but this is to remind you to use only glass or stainless steel or enamel utensils—not ordinary metals.

## Sourdough Starter

1 tsp active dry yeast
¼ cup warm water
¾ cup milk, room temperature
1 cup all-purpose flour (never self-rising flour)

1. In a large glass mixing bowl, dissolve yeast in warm water.
2. Add milk, stirring with a wooden spoon.
3. Gradually stir in the flour, beating until smooth.
4. Cover with plastic wrap and let it stand in a warm, draft-free spot (80° F. to 85° F.) until starter begins to ferment, about 24 hours. The oven is an ideal place. A gas pilot light gives just enough heat. Or turn on the electric oven to the lowest point, heat for a minute or two, then turn it off. Repeat this procedure occasionally.
5. Keep the oven door closed, except to check

progress occasionally. Fermentation is taking place when bubbles form on the surface of the starter, perhaps even before the 24 hours. If the starter does not show fermentation within that time, discard it and start again.

6. When fermentation has begun, pour starter into a wide-mouthed glass quart jar. Stir well and cover tightly with plastic wrap. Let it stand until foamy, 1 or 2 days. When it becomes foamy, stir well and screw on a tight-fitting lid. Store in the refrigerator. When clear liquid has risen to the top, starter is ready for use. Stir down.

7. After using part of the starter (in bread, for example), reserve the remainder and "feed" it in the glass jar by adding equal amounts of flour and milk (cool, not cold). Let the milk stand at room temperature for an hour before adding it to the starter. Beat well with a wooden spoon.

8. Leave the replenished starter uncovered at room temperature until bubbles appear (foamy), up to 12 hours, then refrigerate.

9. Use this starter regularly for bread or pancakes. Remove from refrigerator about an hour before using so it is at room temperature. If you're a real sourdough fan, double the amount of milk and flour added after each use so you will always have enough starter on hand for your baking needs. However, keep it in 2 bottles or it will run over—in spite of the lid. This demonstrates that the starter possesses strength. Use the starter, then feed it at least every 2 weeks to keep it alive and well.

"Plan your work—
work your plan."
Anonymous

# Sourdough White Bread

(See photograph on page 63)

*Yield: 2 loaves*

**Pre-mixing sponge, to be mixed and set aside for several hours before making bread:**

½ cup sourdough starter
2 ½ cups all-purpose flour
2 cups warm water

1. In a large glass mixing bowl and with a wooden spoon, mix starter with flour and warm water. Beat sponge vigorously until smooth.
2. Replenish starter by adding 1 cup of milk (room temperature) and 1 cup of all-purpose flour. Beat until smooth; let stand uncovered at room temperature for about 12 hours, until bubbly and liquid appears on top. Then screw on the lid and refrigerate for the next use.
3. Cover the pre-mixing sponge with plastic wrap and let it stand in a warm, draft-free place (the unheated oven is ideal) for 8 to 12 hours. I usually do this at night and make bread the next morning, or I start the pre-mixing sponge in the morning and bake bread for dinner.

**When sponge is bubbly, proceed with the following ingredients and instructions:**

2 tsps active dry yeast (not imperative but gives the bread a nice boost)
2 tbsps warm water
4 to 4 ¾ cups all-purpose flour
1 tsp salt
3 tbsps sugar
¼ tsp baking soda
3 tbsps vegetable oil

1. Dissolve yeast in warm water in a cup.
2. Sift together 4 cups flour, salt, sugar, and baking soda.

3. In a large mixing bowl add yeast mixture, oil, and sifted dry ingredients gradually, beating well with wooden spoon until smooth and flour is absorbed.

4. Sprinkle remaining ½ cup flour on kneading surface and knead dough until smooth and elastic, adding flour only to keep from sticking.

5. Return ball of dough to the bowl and cover with plastic wrap.

6. Let rise until double in bulk, about 2 hours. Don't hurry it.

7. Punch down dough and divide in half. This bread can be formed into regular loaves and baked in 8½″ x 4½″ pans, or it can be molded into a ball or an oblong loaf.

8. Let rise until almost double in bulk.

9. Preheat oven to 375° F. to 400° F. (This next is a good step but not absolutely necessary for good bread.) If possible at the beginning of oven heating, put a shallow pan of hot water in the bottom of the oven. When bread goes into the oven, put a brick in the pan of water. The steam created is good for developing crustier bread.

10. When bread is ready to go into the oven, make three slashes diagonally in the top of each loaf with a razor blade or a sharp knife. With pastry brush or spray bottle, baste loaves with cold water. Bake on middle rack of the oven. Two or three times during baking, repeat the basting.

11. Bake about 40 to 45 minutes, or until loaves sound hollow when tapped with knuckles. A lower temperature and longer baking develops crustiness, as does baking on tiles (see page 56).

12. Turn out onto wire racks to cool.

**Tip:** If bread is not consumed while fresh, reheat by wrapping in foil and placing it in the oven for 15 minutes at about 350° F. until heated through. Bread will seem to be freshly baked.

## VARIATION:

Substitute 2 tsps of dimalt for the sugar. Add it to the water while yeast is dissolving.

# Sourdough Half-and-Half Bread

*Yield: 2 loaves*

**Pre-mixing sponge, to be mixed and set aside for several hours before making bread:**

1 cup sourdough starter
1 cup milk
2 cups whole wheat flour

1. In large glass mixing bowl and with wooden spoon, mix starter with flour and milk. Beat sponge vigorously until smooth.

2. Replenish starter by adding 1 cup of milk (room temperature) and 1 cup all-purpose flour. Beat until smooth and let stand uncovered at room temperature for about 12 hours, until bubbly and water begins to appear on top. Then screw on the lid and refrigerate for the next use.

3. Cover the pre-mixing sponge in the bowl with plastic wrap and set in a warm, draft-free spot, such as the oven. Let it stand 8 to 12 hours.

**When sponge is bubbly, proceed with the following ingredients and instructions:**

1 ¾ cups milk
2 tbsps butter
¼ cup honey
1 tbsp active dry yeast
¼ cup warm water
¼ tsp sugar
1 cup whole wheat flour
1 tbsp salt
½ tsp baking soda
¼ cup wheat germ (optional)
3 ½ to 4 ½ cups all-purpose flour

1. Scald milk.

2. Remove from burner and add butter and honey, which will cool milk sufficiently when butter melts.

3. Dissolve yeast with sugar in ¼ cup warm water in a cup or small bowl.

4. Sift together 1 cup whole wheat flour with salt and soda.

5. To sourdough mixture which has set for hours, add wheat germ and stir.

6. Add yeast mixture, milk mixture, and sifted dry ingredients. Beat well, adding enough all-purpose flour to make a soft dough.

7. Turn out onto floured surface and knead 8 to 10 minutes, adding more flour as necessary.

8. Divide in half and form loaves. Place in greased pans 8½″ x 4½″ or knead into oblong or round loaves and bake on cookie sheets.

9. Let rise until almost double, but don't let it get too light.

10. Punch down and re-form loaves.

11. Let rise until almost double (3¼″ on rising gauge). Bake in preheated oven at 375° F. to 400° F., 35 to 40 minutes or until done.

12. Remove from oven when done and turn out onto wire rack to cool.

# 100% Whole Wheat Sourdough Bread

(See photograph on page 63)

*Yield: 3 loaves,*

**Pre-mixing sponge, to be mixed and set aside for several hours before making bread:**

1 cup sourdough starter
1 cup milk, room temperature
2 cups whole wheat flour

1. In a large glass mixing bowl and with a wooden spoon, mix starter with flour and milk. Beat sponge vigorously until smooth.

2. Replenish starter by adding 1 cup of milk (room temperature) and 1 cup all-purpose flour. Beat until smooth and let stand uncovered at room temperature for about 12 hours, until bubbly and liquid begins to appear on top. Then screw on the lid and refrigerate for the next use.

3. Cover the pre-mixing sponge in the bowl with plastic wrap and set in a warm, draft-free spot, such as the oven. Let it stand 8 to 12 hours.

**When sponge is bubbly, proceed with the following ingredients and instructions:**

2 cups warm water (115° F.)
1 tbsp active dry yeast
¼ cup honey, sugar, or molasses
2 tbsps butter or vegetable oil
1 tbsp salt
½ tsp baking soda
6 to 7 cups whole wheat flour

1. Pour warm water into a large mixing bowl. Add yeast and sweetening and let yeast dissolve.

2. When yeast is dissolved, add butter, salt, baking soda, and 1 cup whole wheat flour. Beat well with wooden spoon.

3. Add sourdough mixture which has set for hours. Beat vigorously until smooth.

4. Add enough whole wheat flour gradually to make a soft dough. Turn out onto lightly floured surface and knead 8 to 10 minutes, adding more flour as necessary to prevent sticking, until a soft ball is formed.

5. Divide into three portions. Shape into round or oblong or conventional loaves and place in pans or on greased back of a cookie sheet. Let rise until double.

6. Punch down and re-form loaves.

7. When double in bulk a second time, slash tops and bake 30 to 40 minutes at 375° F. to 400° F. or until it tests done.

8. Turn out onto wire rack to cool.

# Sourdough Buns

(See photograph on page 63)

*Yield: About 4 dozen buns*

Use any of the preceding sourdough bread recipes and proceed as follows:

1.  Instead of forming the dough into loaves, squeeze off balls about 1½" to 2" in diameter and place on the greased back of a baking sheet, leaving room for the buns to rise.
2.  Cover with plastic wrap while rising until almost double in bulk.
3.  Bake 20 to 25 minutes at 375° F. to 400° F. If using two baking sheets, just let the second pan continue to rise while the first is baking.

Serve hot or cold.

**Tip:** Leftover buns can be wrapped in foil and reheated in oven at 350° F. about 15 minutes. They will be restored almost to their original soft inside and crispy crust. Or place buns in a Presto cooker on the stove burner for a few minutes. Heat at medium temperature without water in the bottom of the cooker.

# Sourdough Banana Bread

*Yield: 2 medium-sized loaves*

1 ½ cups sourdough starter
1 cup all-purpose flour
1 tsp salt
1 tsp baking soda
2 medium-sized ripe bananas
⅓ cup butter
½ cup sugar
¼ cup molasses
1 egg
½ cup coconut
1 cup nuts, chopped

1.  Let sourdough starter set in a bowl at room temperature at least an hour.

2.  Replenish sourdough starter as explained in previous yeast sourdough bread recipes. Remember, cool (not cold) milk.
3.  Spoon flour to measure it, then sift together twice the flour, salt, and soda.
4.  In mixer bowl, mash bananas.
5.  Add butter, sugar, molasses, and egg; cream well with beater.
6.  Add sourdough starter and sifted dry ingredients. Mix well.
7.  Fold in coconut and nuts and pour into 2 greased loaf pans 7½" x 3½".
8.  Bake in preheated oven at 350° F. to 375° F. for 30 to 35 minutes, or until inserted toothpick comes out clean.
9.  Let stand in pans 5 minutes, then turn out on wire rack to cool.

**Tip:** This bread is best eaten fresh. If it is held over, however, do not wrap in plastic. It becomes wet and undesirable. Instead, wrap in a clean dishtowel; it retains its moistness amazingly. It makes yummy toast.

*QUICK & EASY*
# Sourdough Waffles

*Yield: 4, depending on size*

1 cup sourdough starter
1 cup milk
1 ½ cups all-purpose flour
½ tsp salt
1 tsp baking powder
2 tbsps sugar
3 eggs, separated
⅓ cup vegetable oil

1.  If possible, take sourdough starter and milk from refrigerator at least an hour before using to attain room temperature.
2.  Replenish sourdough starter as explained in previous yeast sourdough bread recipes.
3.  Sift flour, salt, baking powder, and sugar together twice.
4.  Preheat waffle iron.

5. Separate eggs and beat whites to stiff peaks. Set aside. Beat yolks in mixing bowl. Add sourdough starter, milk, and oil; beat together with wooden spoon.
6. Add sifted dry ingredients.
7. Fold in beaten egg whites.
8. With a cup, pour onto hot waffle iron about ½ cup or a little more of batter.
9. Bake waffles at 350° F. to 375° F. until heat goes off and no steam is escaping.
10. Serve with apple sauce or butter and syrup. A special treat is sliced strawberries and whipped cream. Slice berries and sprinkle a little sugar over them. Chill a half hour or so before serving. Delicious and festive! Also check the "Cook's Corner" under the whole wheat waffle recipe on page 71 for Mary's Strawberry Sundae Waffles.

**Tip:** Leftover waffles can be frozen. Pop them into the toaster before serving.

## VARIATIONS:

1. Substitute whole wheat flour for the white flour but remove 1 tbsp of the total measurement of wheat flour.

2. *Pancakes:* Add ½ cup more milk to the above recipe.

"*There is no failure save in giving up.*"
Anonymous

# Breads for Celiacs

(For an explanation of any unfamiliar ingredients listed in these recipes, see the discussion on Ingredients in the last section of this book.)

Because celiac disease is so closely related to bread consumption, a brief discussion seems to be in order. I have made conscientious attempts (with apparent success) to supply the bread needs of friends with the disease. Although the disease is unknown to most people, it is nonetheless real and very distressing to those who have it. Only recently has it been successfully diagnosed and treated—with diet.

Celiac disease goes by many names: Celiac Sprue, gluten sensitive enteropathy, non-tropical sprue and idiopathic steatorrhea, according to a pamphlet from the Gluten Intolerance Group, P.O. Box 23053, Seattle, Washington 98102. The group was formed to assist families in dealing with this difficult disease.

When a person suffers from this disease, it is because the small intestine lining is damaged by gluten, which is the elastic protein substance giving cohesiveness to bread dough. Gluten contains an acid protein called gliadin. The normal intestine has hair-like projections called villi which aid in food digestion; in a celiac, the body's immune system attacks the gliadin and at the same time destroys the villi. This prevents absorption of food through the intestine, especially fats and fat-soluble vitamins A, D, and K.

Usually the disease is diagnosed in young children but there is actually no age limit. It becomes a lifelong disease, with the patient having to live within strict dietary restrictions. When gluten is eliminated from the diet, the patient usually enjoys good health; however, gluten is present in so many foods that a celiac must forever read the labels on all commercial products.

Grains are so much a part of our diet that even a slight amount of gluten in the thickening of a can of cream-style corn, for example, can trigger illness. Gluten is present in wheat, rye, barley, triticale, and oats.

Since gluten is the necessary property for making bread cohesive and elastic, a celiac can never enjoy a sandwich or a piece of toast. Recipes given to celiacs are not very satisfactory; they utilize rice flour, cornmeal, cornstarch, millet, and soya flour. One friend said of the recipes given to her by the doctor, "If I want to eat bread, it's either cement or crumbs in a bowl."

Since several of my friends are celiacs, I began experimenting with some of the flours listed in the preceding paragraph and have developed some recipes which they praise highly. One friend said, after sampling my non-gluten yeast bread, "I didn't know what I craved. It's the yeast in bread. I love this. My literature tells me that yeast isn't successful with these flours. But you've done it."

She suffered no ill effects, nor did the several people who sampled my tests and expressed their reactions. I have tried to pack the small loaves with as much protein as possible because protein is a serious deficiency in the diets lacking grain protein.

Two non-gluten recipes are given here, one using yeast for leavening and the other with baking powder and soda. Variations are also included.

An alarming number of people (in addition to celiacs) are allergic to whole wheat flour but can eat white flour. Still others cannot tolerate any wheat flour but can safely consume rye, barley, and oats which contain low gluten. For this more liberal group I include low-gluten recipes with variations—one using yeast and one with baking powder and soda for leavening.

# Gluten-Free Bread with Yeast

(See photograph on page 64)

*Yield: 2 medium-sized loaves*

2 cups buttermilk
2 tbsps gelatin
2 tbsps active dry yeast
2 tbsps dough conditioner
4 tbsps molasses
¼ cup millet
½ cup rice flour
½ cup cornmeal
¼ cup cornstarch
¼ cup soya flour
¼ tsp soda
1 tsp salt
¾ cup potato granules
2 tbsps vegetable oil
1 egg, beaten, or 2 tbsps lecithin
½ tsp almond extract
½ tsp anise extract
1 tsp caraway seeds (optional)
2 tbsps sesame seeds (optional)
¼ cup or more sunflower seeds (optional)
½ cup almonds, ground in blender (optional)

1. In 3-quart saucepan, heat buttermilk to 115° F. (Use this saucepan for mixing the whole recipe.)
2. With wire whip, beat in gelatin, then add yeast, dough conditioner, and molasses.
3. While yeast is dissolving, grind millet in blender.
4. Sift together twice rice flour, cornmeal, cornstarch, soya flour, millet, soda, and salt. Set aside.
5. With wire whip, add potato granules gradually to yeast mixture.
6. Add oil, egg or lecithin, flavorings, and caraway seeds and beat.
7. Add sifted dry ingredients gradually and mix well. Let rise about an hour for "soaking" of flours.
8. Punch down and spoon into two pans 7½″ x 3½″. Dip a clean spoon in water, then press down the dough, smoothing surface.
9. Let rise in pans about ½ hour.
10. Bake 35 to 40 minutes at 375° F. to 400° F.
11. Remove from oven. Let stand in pans about 5 minutes, then turn out onto wire rack to cool.

**Tip:** If using dried buttermilk, sift 5 tbsps of buttermilk powder with flours and use warm water for the liquid instead of cultured buttermilk.

**Tip:** Sweet milk can be substituted for buttermilk. Proceed the same except eliminate soda and use 1 tsp baking powder (Rumford's).

**Tip:** Potato powder or granules is necessary for these celiac recipes. Potato *flakes* will not work for this recipe, nor does potato *flour*, even when twice as much is used. Potato powder is harder to find than potato flakes. Potato flour must be purchased in the health food store. I can find potato powder only in large cans under the name of "Instant Mashed Potatoes." Potato flakes are also listed as instant mashed potatoes. To make sure you are getting the right product, shake the can or package. If it rattles and is lightweight, it is flakes. The powder is much, much heavier and doesn't make a similar rattling sound at all. Although it is much more expensive than flakes, the powder will last a long time.

**Tip:** If time schedule is tight, mix at night and refrigerate in loaf pans and bake in the morning without a first rise as detailed in the instructions. This means the bread rises only once in pans for about 8 hours.

**Tip:** This bread freezes well. Slice cooled loaf before freezing so that 1 or 2 slices can be removed as needed.

# Gluten-Free Bread (Non-Yeast)

*Yield: 2 loaves*

1 tbsp gelatin
½ cup hot water
¾ cup potato powder
4 tbsps molasses or honey
2 tbsps vegetable oil
1 egg
1 tsp almond flavoring
1 ½ cups cold buttermilk
¼ cup millet, ground in blender
½ cup rice flour
½ cup cornmeal
¼ cup soya flour
¼ cup cornstarch
1 tsp soda
1 ½ tsps baking powder (Rumford's)
1 tsp salt
2 tbsps sesame seeds (optional)
¼ cup sunflower seeds (optional)
grated rind of half a lemon or orange (optional)

1. With wire whip, beat gelatin in hot water in a small mixing bowl and add potato powder, beating well.
2. Pour buttermilk, molasses, oil, egg, and flavorings into large mixing bowl. Add gelatin mixture, beating well with slotted spoon.
3. Grind millet in blender and sift with rice flour, cornmeal, soya flour, cornstarch, soda, baking powder, and salt. Add to liquid mixture in bowl and beat well with spoon.
4. Add options as desired.
5. Spoon into 2 greased loaf pans (7 ½″ x 3 ½″). Smooth tops with spoon, dipped in water, to keep dough from sticking to it.
6. Bake in preheated oven 350° F. to 375° F. for 35 to 45 minutes.
7. Remove from oven. Let stand in pans 5 minutes. Turn out onto wire rack to cool.
8. This bread can be sliced and frozen. Remove 1 or 2 slices at a time, as needed.

# Low-Gluten Wheat-Free Bread (Yeast and Buttermilk)

*Yield: 2 loaves*

1 ¼ cups buttermilk
2 tbsps gelatin
2 tbsps active dry yeast
2 tbsps dough conditioner
4 tbsps molasses
⅓ cup millet
⅓ cup barley
⅓ cup buckwheat
⅓ cup oats
⅓ cup rye flour
⅓ cup rice flour
¼ cup cornmeal
¼ cup soya flour
1 tsp salt
¼ tsp soda
½ cup potato powder
2 tbsps vegetable oil
1 egg, beaten, or 2 tbsps lecithin
½ tsp anise flavoring (optional)
½ tsp almond flavoring (optional)
1 tsp caraway seeds
2 tbsps sesame seeds
grated rind of half an orange or lemon (optional)

1. This whole recipe can be mixed in a 3-quart saucepan. Heat buttermilk to 115° F. in saucepan. Remove from heat.
2. With wire whip, stir in gelatin to dissolve.
3. Add yeast, dough conditioner, and molasses. Set aside.
4. While yeast is dissolving, grind millet in blender, then grind oats, buckwheat, and barley on highest speed.
5. Sift the flours (millet, oats, buckwheat, barley, rye, rice, cornmeal, and soya) together twice with salt and soda. Set aside.
6. To yeast mixture in saucepan add oil, egg or lecithin, flavorings, and seeds.
7. Add potato powder, beating with wire whip for smoothness.

8. Add sifted dry ingredients gradually and mix well. Add options, as desired.
9. Let rise about an hour.
10. Punch down and spoon into two greased pans 7½″ x 3½″. Dip a spoon in water and press down, smoothing surface of loaves.
11. Let rise in pans about an hour and bake 35 to 40 minutes at 375° F. to 400° F.
12. Remove from oven. Let stand in pans 5 to 10 minutes and turn out onto wire rack to cool.

**Tip:** If you don't like caraway, substitute almond flavoring for anise and grind about ½ cup almonds in blender. This imparts a delicious flavor as well as providing additional protein.

**Tip:** If using dried buttermilk instead of liquid buttermilk, sift 5 tbsps buttermilk powder with flours and use warm water for liquid.

**Tip:** If time schedule is tight, mix at night, refrigerate in loaf pans after completing through step 9. Next morning remove from refrigerator and place in preheated oven. Bake 50 to 60 minutes at 375° F. to 400° F.

**Tip:** This bread freezes well. Slice the loaf before freezing it so 1 or 2 slices can be removed as needed and the bread will not become stale.

## VARIATION:

Sweet milk can be substituted for buttermilk; soda must be eliminated. Proceed in the same manner otherwise.

# Low-Gluten Wheat-Free Bread (Non-Yeast)

(See photograph on page 64)

*Yield: 2 loaves*

1 ¾ cups milk
2 tbsps gelatin
⅓ cup honey or molasses
½ cup potato powder, or ½ cup leftover mashed potatoes
1 egg

2 tbsps vegetable oil
1 tsp anise flavoring
1 tsp caraway seeds, or 1 tsp almond flavoring and ½ cup almonds ground in blender
⅓ cup millet
⅓ cup oats
⅓ cup buckwheat
⅓ cup barley
⅓ cup rice flour or rice mix
⅓ cup rye flour
¼ cup cornmeal
¼ cup soya flour
1 tsp salt
2 tsps baking powder (Rumford's)
¼ cup sunflower seeds (optional)
grated rind of an orange or a lemon (optional)

1. This whole recipe can be mixed in a 3-quart saucepan. Scald milk in saucepan. Remove from heat.
2. With wire whip, gradually beat in gelatin to dissolve.
3. Add sweetening and potato powder. Beat well with whip.
4. Add egg, oil, flavoring, and caraway. Beat well.
5. Grind millet, oats, buckwheat, and barley in blender on high speed.
6. Sift together twice all flours with cornmeal, salt, and baking powder. Add to mixture in pan. Beat well with spoon.
7. Add options, if desired.
8. Pour into 2 greased loaf pans 7½″ x 3½″. Smooth tops with spoon.
9. Bake in preheated oven 35 to 45 minutes at 350° F. to 375° F.
10. Remove from oven and let stand in pans for 5 minutes. Turn out onto wire rack to cool.

**Tip:** This bread can be frozen. Slice first, then you can remove only 1 or 2 slices as needed.

# Things You Need and Things You Need to Know

## Equipment

Basic tools of the trade are necessary for a successful home baker. Some are absolutely essential, while others are nice to have when you branch out into all the facets of the recipes included in this book. Use this as your shopping list, acquiring the bare essentials first, then adding more as the budget permits.

Saucepans, one-, two-, and three-quart
Skillets, large and small
Mixing bowls (very large, medium, and small) with sloping sides
Large bread bowl or pan for mixing (about 6-quart). Plastic with tight-fitting lid is ideal.
Flour sifter
2 or 3 large flexible paper plates with fluted 1-inch sides for sifting dry ingredients—a real time-saver. Keep in plastic bag with sifter in cupboard.
Ball-bearing rotary eggbeater or electric handbeater
Wire whip, small and large
Rubber spatulas or scrapers
Flexible metal spatula or pancake turner
Slotted spoon, plastic or metal
Wooden spoon
Straight-edged knife for "leveling off" dry ingredients or small spatula
Sharp knife for cutting dough and slashing tops of loaves
Pizza cutter
Serrated sawtooth bread knife
Measuring cups for dry ingredients ("measure line" even with top) 1 pint, 1 cup, ½ cup, ⅓ cup, ¼ cup
Measuring cup for liquids (with extra rim above "cup line")
Measuring spoons—¼ tsp, ½ tsp, 1 tsp, 1 tbsp

Muffin tins (preferably 2 which hold 1 dozen each)
2 wire racks which permit air circulation underneath for cooling
Pastry brushes, long and short handle
Spray bottle
Timer
Pot holders
Rolling pin
Pastry sock for rolling pin
Pastry cloth or canvas cover for breadboard[1]
Cookie sheets
4 or 5 loaf tins, about 8 ½ " x 4 ½ " x 2 ¾ " (inside top measurement)—do not buy the wider pans
Dripper pan about 8" or 9" x 12" x 2 ¼ "
Square pan, 8" or 9"
Can opener
Vegetable parer
Cutting board
Ruler
Thermometers, both "oven" and "candy"
Breadboard for kneading, or use clean tabletop
Blender
Electric mixer or heavy-duty bread mixer[2]
Electric grain grinder[3]

**Tip:** A large (46-oz.) juice can, with one end neatly removed, is fine for baking raisin-nut or date-nut bread, or just plain bread. Cut two circles of foil the size of the can. Place one in the bottom of the can and grease it. Form ball of dough and drop into well-greased can without pressing down. Can should be half full of dough. Put another circle of foil on top of the dough. Let rise until double in bulk. Set cans standing up, in the oven. Allow at least 15 minutes longer baking time than when baking in loaf pans.

Vegetable cans (16 oz.) can also be used for small loaves.

**Tip:** For crusty breads, unglazed tiles are wonderful. Or try an "Old Stone Pizza Kit" or a similar product which can be found in some specialty shops.

For French Bread, rising cradles are excellent. Tiles and cradles can be purchased by mail order through Lilian DeLong, 293 E. 1100 North, Centerville, UT 84014 for $19.50 postpaid.

1. CANVAS COVERS: A soft dough, which makes better bread and rolls, can best be handled with a canvas-covered kneading board. A pastry cloth is available in the kitchenware department of some hardware stores, as is a pastry sock for the rolling pin. If one is not available, make your own. Construct a casing like a pillowcase out of lightweight canvas. Measure the length and width of the board to be covered (or a piece of heavy corrugated cardboard will do), allowing 3 to 4 inches for shrinkage. French seam all raw edges to prevent fraying. Slip this cover over the breadboard and sprinkle lightly with flour for rolling, kneading, or molding bread, rolls, pastry dough or rolled cookies.

Once you have used these aids, you'll never be without them. The cover and sock may be used several times between launderings if kept in a plastic bag in the refrigerator.

2. MIXERS: Small electric handbeaters will be overtaxed when mixing stiff doughs as for bread. Several electric mixers (such as the Mixmaster) are readily available, priced at about $100. Of course, these mixers can be used for all kinds of beating and mixing from egg whites to bread *sponges*, but will not handle bread dough stiff enough to form into loaves. The instructions in most of the recipes in this book are geared to this kind of a mixer simply because they are not as expensive as a heavy-duty electric bread mixer and therefore would already be in more homes.

The Braun, Bosch, Kenwood, and Blakesley are the principal heavy-duty bread mixers, all equal in power. These are popular in the West; no doubt there are others in other parts of the country. The Braun is the least expensive, priced at just over $200, with the Bosch, Blakesley, and Kenwood over $300. Attachments are available for each, such as a blender, a salad maker, etc. A bread mixer is a timesaver and produces the best results because not as much flour must be added as when kneading dough by hand, thus ensuring a softer dough.

Investigate bread mixers thoroughly before buying. They are made in different sizes and for different needs. Get one that suits *you*. Bread mixers can be found in hardware and specialty shops or dealers. Or, make mail inquiries to any or all of the following outlets:

Platt Mill & Mix, 3068 Highland Drive, Salt Lake City, UT 84106, handles several mixers. They have the U.S. franchise for Braun.

Magic Mill International Headquarters, 235 West 200 South, Salt Lake City, UT 84101

Grover's, 330 W. University Dr., Tempe, AZ 85281

Kitchenetics Corp., 1450 Dell Ave., Campbell, CA 95008

3. HOME GRINDERS OR GRAIN MILLS: If you have a large family, a home flour mill will save a lot of money when you grind your own wheat instead of buying flour in the store. There is also an added bonus of freshness, which results in better flavor and higher nutrition. Remember! These are long-term investments. Investigate before buying. New mills are always entering the market. Not all remain. See demonstrations of several and use the flour before deciding. Don't be rushed or pushed. This is *your* investment with which you will live a long time. Get what you want, then *use* it.

If you have health problems, such as celiac disease, which require the use of various grains other than wheat, for economy's sake invest in a home mill, rather than buying expensive commercially produced specialty flours. One word of warning for this situation: soy, rice, and sweet corn, in particular, contain considerable oil and might "gum up" an ordinary home machine. Determine from the representative if corn can be safely ground, being a large grain. Ask specific questions of your demonstrator. Then be sure to keep the mill cleaned out with a brush or blower end of a vacuum cleaner. Weevils are a problem when a mill is not in frequent operation. Always be sure to clean it after a period of disuse.

Inquire by mail from the following good home-mill sources:

Platt Mill & Mix, 3068 Highland Drive, Salt Lake City, UT 84106 (Handles 10 different mills.)

Magic Mill International Headquarters, 235 West 200 South, Salt Lake City, UT 84101

Grover's, 330 W. University Dr., Tempe, AZ 85281

Lee Engineering Co., 2023 W. Wisconsin Ave., Milwaukee, WI 53233

Kitchenetics Corp., 1450 Dell Ave., Campbell, CA 95008

# Ingredients

## YEAST

Leavening used today is of two types: yeast and powders, such as baking powder, baking soda, and cream of tartar.

Yeasts increase "budding." They are among the simplest kinds of plants and belong to the fungi family. Combined with sweeteners, yeast ferments, causing the rising power in bread dough. Mixing or kneading distributes the little gaseous bubbles throughout the dough mass to make it light and porous. It is a fermented leavener.

Yeast as we know it today has evolved from unreliable homemade kinds to a product easily marketed and stored. Compressed yeast can be purchased in tiny cakes (.6 oz.) or in large one-pound cakes available in some bakeries. This yeast can be stored only a short time in the refrigerator.

Active dry yeast has, for the most part, replaced the compressed yeast because of ease of packaging, storing, and marketing, and is available in ¼ oz. foil envelopes which contain slightly more than ¾ tablespoon of yeast. *Be sure to read date lines.* A larger jar (4 oz.) is also available. Two-pound containers can be purchased at many supermarkets. If they are not readily available, ask the manager to procure them for you. The two-pound container which holds 128 tablespoons of yeast, is a real economy. Since the recipes in this book require full tablespoons of yeast, using the ¼ oz. package, which contains slightly less than a tablespoonful, will not give exactly the same results.

The yeast measurements in these recipes are on the high side of the scale. If you are constantly at home and can allow for longer rising periods, a little less yeast (one tablespoon instead of two) will suffice. However, with my testing, I have kept in mind the bread baker on the run to whom an hour means more than the price of a tablespoon of yeast. Also remember that yeast is nutrition; hence, a larger amount of yeast means greater nutrition.

Also please check "Altitude Adjustments" later in this section.

Rapid-mix, no-dissolve yeast called "baker's yeast" is now obtainable. The French product is under the name brand "Saf-Instant"; the German product is "Fermipan." Both are available in the United States. These yeasts, which need not be dissolved, are added *with the flour*, thereby saving time. "Instant Blend Yeast," packaged in small envelopes in supermarkets, is a similar product and is also added with the flour.

Saf-Instant and Fermipan require only about half the quantity of conventional active dry yeast, and the action is a little faster. These yeasts are listed with some "food plans" and are available in some food-storage outlets.

As this book goes to press, a brand-new product called Fleischmann's RapidRise yeast has appeared on supermarket shelves in foil envelopes. The label states that it's 50 percent faster! This, too, is a yeast which is mixed in the flour instead of being dissolved in liquids. All liquids are heated together to 130 degrees and added to the yeast-flour mixture in the mixing bowl, then stirred and kneaded. In many of the recipes in this book I have instructed bread bakers to mold the loaves, place them in the pans, and let them rise until double in volume, then to reknead the loaves and let them rise again before baking. This develops excellent texture. I have discovered that the new yeast can be used with only one rise in the pans, producing a good loaf, although not as fine in texture as with two rises in the pan. Bread can actually be prepared in a bread mixer and baked in just a little over one hour with RapidRise! Using the same method of heating all liquids together to 130° F., you can achieve comparable results with "baker's yeast" (Saf-Instant or Fermipan). However, this cannot be done with all of these recipes. Add your own notes by the recipes, especially when using new yeasts, so you will know those most adaptable to your schedule.

In addition to this RapidRise yeast, Red Star has just come out with a new yeast in two-pound packages which feel like bricks, very similar to Saf-Instant and Fermipan. When the package is opened, however, the yeast relaxes like other yeast products. The label instructs the bread baker to use only 40 percent of the amount of ordinary active dry yeast. If it is not in your supermarket, ask the manager to stock it. Follow instructions on the package for preservation and use. Adjust the instructions in the recipes in this book to whatever yeast you are using. Believe it or not, it isn't all that complicated.

Because of ready access to active dry yeast, the recipes in this book have been tested with it, and measurements given are for that kind of yeast. When using the large two-pound container of regular active dry yeast, I transfer the contents to smaller jars with tight-fitting lids and freeze the yeast, using one jar at a time. I always keep large containers as part of my food storage. In the original can or package yeast will store at least a year in a cool, dry storage area. I store mine in the freezer, marking the purchase date on the container for rotation.

### Using Yeast

Most books and recipes tell you to have yeast at room temperature before putting it into warm or lukewarm water. This always causes a delay. From long experience I have learned to use it directly from the freezer, having the water warmer (115° F.).

The temperature of liquid is important. If the water is too cool, yeast activity is very slow. A *minimum* temperature of 78° F. is necessary for activation. However, yeast is destroyed when the temperature is as high as 140° F. This still leaves considerable latitude between those two figures. Do not depend on finger testing water; invest in a good thermometer. With a candy thermometer I actually test the temperature and add yeast to 115° F. liquid. You'll be surprised how warm this feels to the touch. Use a thermometer at least until your touch has been trained.

### Emergency Activation of Yeast

If the yeast does not activate normally, drop about 1/8 teaspoonful of ginger into the yeast mixture; this nudges activation. If the yeast still refuses to activate, don't use it at all. The bread will not rise properly, so don't waste all the other ingredients. The yeast could be dead, although it seldom is. The problem usually occurs because water is too cool or too hot.

### Sourdough Start

Still another fermented leavener is a sourdough start (see Sourdough Starter recipe on page 75), which imparts a "sour" taste to products.

## BAKING POWDER, BAKING SODA, AND CREAM OF TARTAR

*Baking powder* is generally used in baking cakes and quick breads to be immediately popped into the oven, requiring no extra "rising" time. Most baking powder now available is "double-acting," which means that rising happens in two steps, once when liquid is added (in the mixing) and once when the bread is put into the oven heat. Quick bread, made with double-acting baking powder, can be mixed ahead of time, refrigerated, then baked later just before serving.

Most double-acting baking powder contains aluminum sulfate, a chemical which can be harmful to the human system. (Read the labels.) Rumford's Baking Powder, purchased at health food stores, is probably the only safe double-acting baking powder on the market. It does not contain aluminum sulfate. There are one or two brands of single-acting baking powder on the market. However, you can make your own single-acting baking powder, as follows:

For one teaspoon of single-acting baking powder, use ½ tsp cream of tartar, ¼ tsp sodium bicarbonate, ¼ tsp cornstarch or arrowroot.

When using single-acting baking powder, for good leavening action mix the ingredients quickly and get the bread or cake immediately into the oven.

*Baking powder* is used when a recipe calls for sweet non-acidic ingredients, such as sweet milk.

*Baking soda* must be used for leavening when a recipe calls for acidic ingredients, such as buttermilk, yogurt, sour milk, sour cream, fruit juices, or molasses.

*Cream of tartar*, derived from grapes, is also a leavener, but not double-acting.

Because baking powder and baking soda are high in sodium, and therefore adverse to health, the use of baking powder and baking soda should be curtailed as much as possible.

## LIQUIDS

*Water* is perhaps the most commonly used liquid in bread. Usually I prefer using water instead of milk, because the flavor of the bread is enhanced. If you want milk, drink it while enjoying a slice of tasty bread and butter.

*Milk* promotes a softer texture to breads and also adds protein and calcium. Dried milk can be sifted with flour.

Many recipes call for scalded milk. Before pasteurization became standard procedure, scalding the milk was necessary to destroy bacteria, which might cause dough to sour. This is not true today with pasteurized milk. "Scalding" milk is simply heating it in a pan on the stove until little bubbles form around the edge and surface. I honestly think that scalding the milk for rolls, for example, improves the texture of the finished product, but it could be my imagination. Scalded milk must be cooled somewhat before being added to the other ingredients. Again, use a thermometer.

*Potato water* adds flavor as well as mild leavening to the dough. It promotes yeast growth and improves the texture. Why not boil potatoes in an excessive amount of water and save the water in a glass jar and refrigerate it for breadmaking, as needed? In a recipe, you can substitute potato water for plain water, adding enough hot water from the faucet to make up the total water measurement.

*Buttermilk* and *sour milk* create a superior bread, even if used as only part of the total liquid of a recipe. Since it is acidic, we usually (but not always) use a small amount of baking soda, which can be sifted with flour. Cracks in buttermilk bread are rare and browning is superb. Cut the oven heat slightly unless you enjoy a good dark crust. The texture is excellent. Another advantage to using buttermilk is that it aids digestion.

To save time and extra dishes, I usually heat buttermilk in a saucepan to 120° F. (by the thermometer), remove it from the burner, and add frozen yeast and sweetening as well as butter (if the recipe calls for melted butter). This cools the buttermilk a bit. The butter doesn't melt completely but softens, which is fine for the kneading process. The same thing is true when using sour cream. Ordinarily, fats are added after the yeast has dissolved; however, I have found that this shortcut works very well with buttermilk.

## EGGS

Eggs act as emulsifiers in bread dough, producing a finer texture. They also add a golden color and additional nutrition.

When making yeast rolls and the recipe calls for beaten eggs, don't skimp on the beating. This makes rolls lighter and finer textured.

You can achieve an attractive golden glaze to breads by beating an egg (a tablespoon of water can be added to stretch it if necessary), then brushing it over the tops of the loaves with a pastry brush. Sprinkle on sesame seeds or poppy seeds, if desired, for added attraction.

## FATS AND OILS

Fats and oils are important in keeping bread fresh. Due to economy measures and calorie counting, margarine has become almost interchangeable with butter. But nothing rivals real butter. When a recipe calls for "no substitute" for butter, please comply.

Vegetable oils are used in most of the recipes in this book.

To prevent sticking when kneading whole wheat bread, I use a bit of oil on the kneading surface. However, when I use oil to "grease" bread pans, the bread sometimes sticks, so I use shortening for that purpose.

There are controversies over shortening, lard, and oils which I choose to ignore in this book because it is not a "health book."

## SWEETENERS

Sweeteners are necessary but are subject to individual taste. Honey and molasses not only sweeten but add flavor and start the action of yeast. Molasses also darkens bread. Sorghum, if available, is wonderful. Sugar is sugar. Brown sugar adds a different flavor. Again there are controversies. Raw sugar is now nothing but white sugar with molasses added. Turbinado, a natural sugar, is sold at health food stores at quite a high price. We won't even discuss artificial sweeteners. New sweeteners are always being developed.

Honey or sugar or molasses is often specified in these recipes. If you are using honey, here are some suggestions for substitutions:

1. Use half as much honey as sugar called for in a recipe, or according to individual taste.

2. Honey is liquid, so a little more (perhaps ¼ cup) flour might be needed for proper dough consistency. Because flour is a variable quantity in most bread recipes, this is of little concern.

3. You may find it necessary to lower the oven temperature 25° F. when using honey.

*Wheat for Man: Why and How*, page 10, contains important information concerning honey and its storage.

## DIASTATIC MALT (DIMALT)

Diastatic malt, a natural sweetener, is little known but is marvelous for breadmaking and is the secret of wonderful sugarless bread. A commercial product under the name of Dimalt, produced by Bio-Schiff Food Products, Inc., is available in health food stores. For convenience, therefore, throughout the book diastatic malt (even the homemade kind) will be referred to as dimalt. Dimalt is packed with enzymes and vitamins, which increase bread's nutritional value, and acts as a catalyst to the yeast and flour. However, making dimalt is so easy that you'll want to make your own. The economy of using dimalt instead of honey or sugar is incredible —and don't forget the physical benefits of eliminating sweeteners.

Only one teaspoonful of the powder is necessary in a two-loaf batch of bread. A little more can be used (I use one *tablespoon*), but don't go overboard. This is not a case of a little is good, so more is better. Don't use more than a tablespoonful for two loaves.

Watch the temperature of liquid used with dimalt. Liquid temperature over 110° F. will kill dimalt. Even two degrees makes a difference, so be sure the liquid temperature is 100° F. to 110° F. Learn to use it and you'll be forever grateful. The flavor and texture of bread made with dimalt are excellent. The bread also develops a better crust. Toast from dimalt bread is unsurpassable, whether it be whole wheat or white. Wheat is normally weak in lysine, but with dimalt the protein in the bread is increased by about 5 percent, due partly to the fact that the amino acid lysine is tripled in the sprouting.

Here's how to make your own dimalt: Place one cup of wheat (this is the whole wheat, called wheat berries in some localities) in a widemouthed glass jar. Cover the opening with nylon net or even a discarded nylon hose. Secure it with a rubber band. Fill the jar with water and soak the wheat for about twelve hours. Drain off (but don't discard the water—water your plants with it). After draining, place jar on its side in a plate for air circulation (bottom end of jar should rest on rim of plate so that tilt will cause remaining water to drain). Three times a day, rinse the swelling grain with tepid water to prevent mold from forming. Shake and drain.

A commercial sprouter may also be used for sprouting the wheat kernels.

Continue this procedure for two or three days, only until the little shoots are about the same length as the grains, or a little less. Longer white rootlets form on the other end of the kernel. Remove the sprouted wheat from the jar and arrange it evenly on two large cookie sheets. Set the oven temperature no higher than 150° F. or 200° F. Place the trays in the oven, keeping the oven door ajar with a hot pad so moisture can escape. Dry the sprouts *thoroughly*, eight hours or perhaps a little less. During hot weather they can be dried outdoors in the sun, covered with a net or screen; this process takes longer, of course.

When the sprouts are thoroughly dry, put them in the blender and blend them into powder. If sprouted grain is not *completely* dry, it will not powder well. Store in a glass jar at room temperature. The dimalt does not require special storage treatment. Because so little is needed in bread making, one cup of wheat sprouted, dried, and powdered goes a long way.

## POTATOES

Potatoes add quality and nutrition to a loaf of bread, improving texture, rising ability, and moistness. When I serve mashed potatoes for dinner, I prepare extra and refrigerate the leftovers for the next batch of bread. If mashed potatoes are not available, potato flakes or powder can be added for the same results. With a wire whip, beat the flakes or powder into hot (115° F.) liquid. Sweet potatoes or yams also impart an inimitable color, flavor and texture.

## MILLET

You may look at the tiny round golden balls of millet and turn up your nose, saying, "Bird seed!" True—but it is much more. Millet is a high source of protein (about 9 percent) and is a rich source of trace elements necessary for human nutrition. Stories are told of Chinese armies marching miles without fatigue on a daily ration of millet.

Millet is easily combined with other foods and is also good for the digestive tract. You will, therefore, find millet as an "optional" ingredient in several of these recipes.

Millet can be simmered on low heat and used for a hot cereal or it can be ground in the blender to make a powder for use in bread. Protein in the bread is thereby enhanced.

Millet can be purchased in food storage outlets or even in feed stores or health food stores.

## HERBS, SEEDS, NUTS

Don't be afraid to experiment with herbs, seeds, and nuts. Add them to bread as desired for unusual flavors, additional protein—or additional calories.

Dill is an excellent flavor addition and can simply be added to any bread recipe as desired. A rule of thumb would be to add ½ tsp dill seeds per loaf.

Caraway seeds are a refreshing addition to any bread; use ½ teaspoon per loaf. Caraway seeds are necessary in rye and pumpernickel breads.

With nuts skyrocketing in price, try substitutes. Sunflower seeds are cheaper than walnuts, excellent in flavor and highly nutritious.

Almonds are cheaper than walnuts, the protein contained is high, and the flavor is remarkable. Chop on the coarsest setting on the blender. Part of the almonds are ground almost to powder while bigger chunks remain. Add these to a recipe for variety. A teaspoon of almond flavoring can be added to the recipe to heighten flavor.

## DOUGH CONDITIONERS

Homemade 100 percent whole wheat bread is usually heavier in texture and harder to make successfully than white bread. Dough conditioners help considerably. For example, you can crush vitamin C tablets between two spoons and add it to the water as the bread is started, or you can use powdered vitamin C. This acts as a dough conditioner, resulting in a lighter, more elastic loaf. Use 500 mg. to 1,000 mg. (your preference) per four-loaf recipe.

An excellent commercial "Dough Conditioner" (that's the brand name) can be purchased from Shirley J Foodway, 740 West 1700 South #8, Salt Lake City, UT 84104. This dough conditioner is a combination of whey, cornstarch, vitamin C, emulsifiers, salt, spice and honey.

The dough conditioner works as a yeast enhancer, helping it to achieve its maximum potential. It also strengthens the gluten and produces a lighter, more elastic loaf. Since rising time is hastened, the dough doesn't dry out as much. Send to the above address for the dough conditioner literature and price list.

## SALT

Salt is supposedly necessary for yeast action. However, I have often eliminated salt (sometimes inadvertently) and find that the bread is usually up to standard. Salt is a matter of taste—even a developed taste. In these recipes I have tried to appeal to the average taste, if there is such a thing. Try cutting down as you bake, even from the amounts given in recipes in this book, and see if you can develop a taste for less salt. Salt has been established as a cause of high blood pressure and fluid retention in the body.

## LECITHIN

Lecithin, either liquid or powdered, can be used when specified in a few of the recipes. A soybean product, lecithin is a body lubricator. Powdered lecithin can be sifted with the flour. However, do not try to measure liquid lecithin; simply "guesstimate," because it sticks to everything it touches and is difficult to remove. I buy lecithin by the gallon container and keep a small squeeze bottle of it in the cupboard at room temperature. If the lecithin spills, wipe it up with a paper towel rather than a dishcloth. Store in a cool place. Lecithin can be purchased in health food stores or can be mail ordered from Platt Mill & Mix, as can gluten flour below.

## GLUTEN FLOUR

Gluten flour is also included in a few recipes, especially 100 percent whole wheat products. This can be purchased in pound quantities in most health food stores, but it is quite expensive. Its value in the bread, however, is inestimable. Gluten is the protein part of the wheat kernel.

Concise instructions for making gluten flour from scratch are given in *Wheat for Man: Why and How*, pages 13–14. The information is valuable, but buying gluten flour is quite a convenience.

## WHEY

Whey, a derivative of cheese making, is a cream-colored powder which adds nutrition and sweetness to any bread. Add it as you wish, from a tablespoon up to half a cup to most of the bread recipes. It is not specified in recipes in this book simply because of lack of availability in many localities.

## WHEAT AND FLOURS

High consumption of "fast foods" leaves us without knowledge of what is actually on supermarket shelves. Names of items may differ in different areas. For example, in the West, wheat storage is common. Because of the dry climate, we can buy it from many commercial outlets and we store it by the bushel. In other areas, wheat is called "wheat berries" and is hard to find except in health food stores. However, with a return to basic foods, wheat and other grains are becoming easier to find. I was shocked when a friend, recently from the East, told me she had never seen wheat until she moved to Utah. In damp climates, of course, storage is difficult if not impossible, so it is understandably rare.

Wheat in fifty-pound bags can be purchased from some supermarkets and storage outlets, or directly from mills and feed stores. Caution: seed wheat purchased from feed stores, ordinarily sold for planting, has been *chemically treated*. Never buy that. Buy only wheat which is packaged for human consumption. Buying in quantity is the economical way to supply your family's needs. Store what you eat and eat what you store.

Having good, high-protein wheat on hand is security. Until the wheat kernel is broken, the nutritive value is maintained. Store cleaned wheat in a cool, dark, dry place in airtight containers, either metal or plastic. A good weevil preventive is to pour one cup of salt (rock salt is ideal) in a cloth sack or an old sock tightly tied. Place one of these salt bags in the bottom, pour in the wheat, and place another salt bag on top of the wheat before putting the lid firmly in place. Weevils need moisture for propagation. This is why storage wheat must be low moisture (10 percent or less). The salt draws out the excess moisture from the kernels.

Other flours, such as rye, can be purchased in the supermarket. Soy, rice, oat, and specialty flours can be purchased at health food stores. If the flours are not available, the stores can order them for you.

Wheat flour is available in many forms. Probably the most used flour and least expensive product is all-purpose flour, which can be purchased in five-pound, ten-pound, twenty-five-pound, and fifty-pound sacks. "Bleached" or "unbleached" is usually marked on the bag. Millers tell me conflicting stories about bleached and unbleached flour. Some say the only difference between the two is that an immediate bleach and aging chemical is added to bleached all-purpose flour and is simply left out of unbleached flour. Unbleached flour will whiten and age naturally in a few weeks; the lack of whiteness is not apparent to the untrained eye. Some unbleached flour is not synthetically enriched, as bleached white flour is.

Whatever the flour you use, buy the best. Good baking results require good flour, in my opinion.

*Cake flour* is made from soft spring wheat, is more highly refined than all-purpose and also is more expensive. Do not use it in bread baking. Self-rising flour is also avoided in this book.

*Bread flour* (a brand name of Pillsbury and Gold Medal) is a little higher in protein than plain all-purpose flour. I have had excellent results with this product.

*Whole wheat flour* is available commercially—but do be careful. Some brands of commercial whole wheat flour make heavy bread. So if you have poor results with the first brand you buy, try again. Pillsbury's and General Mills' products are good. Central Milling Co. of Logan, Utah, puts out "Red Rose" whole wheat flour which is excellent. There may be others, too. The Red Rose brand costs considerably less than the big companies' brands and is in economical twenty-five-pound bags.

Commercial whole wheat flour, however, has the disadvantage of not being fresh. Thousands of homemakers, especially in the Mountain West, own home mills for grinding storage wheat into good flour. The flour can be ground just before mixing, with a resulting excellent flavor and preservation of nutrients. The whole kernel is ground. Nothing is discarded; nothing is added. All the nutritive values and the bran are there in freshly ground flour. However, vitamin E oxidizes rapidly so it is a good idea to freeze the flour until needed.

The higher the protein content of the wheat, the better the bread. If you have only storage wheat of 12 percent or less, add gluten flour to your recipe to improve the quality of bread.

## Altitude Adjustments

Altitude affects baking results. The higher the altitude, the less the atmospheric pressure. This means that water which boils at 212° F. at sea level boils at 202° F. at 5,000 feet.

Yeast doughs rise faster at higher elevations. Therefore, a little *less* yeast is required at higher altitudes. If you are using these recipes at an altitude lower than 3,500 feet, use slightly more yeast. For example, if the recipe calls for 2 tablespoons of yeast and you live at a lower elevation, you may have better results by using 2½ or 3 tablespoons.

Adjust baking temperatures slightly higher at higher altitudes. To keep it straight in your mind, simply think: Live higher, lift temperature (or add five minutes to the total baking time). Live lower, lower temperature.

This is one reason two temperatures and two baking times are given in the recipes in this book. The other reason is that every oven differs. Jot notes in your book about what works best for you at your altitude with your oven, then you won't be wondering every time you use a certain recipe.

"A creative mess . . . is better than tidy idleness."

# *Equivalents*

## General (English Conversions)

a pinch or dash = less than 1/8 tsp
3 tsps = 1 tbsp
2 tbsps = 1/8 cup
4 tbsps = ¼ cup
5 tbsps plus 1 tsp = ⅓ cup
8 tbsps = ½ cup
12 tbsps = ¾ cup
16 tbsps = 1 cup
1 liquid ounce = 2 tbsps
½ pint = 1 cup
1 pint = 2 cups
2 pints = 1 quart
4 cups = 1 quart
4 quarts = 1 gallon
8 quarts = 1 peck
4 pecks = 1 bushel
16 ounces = 1 pound
16 liquid ounces = 2 cups
28 grams = 1 ounce
454 grams = 1 pound
4 cups flour = 1 pound
1 cup white flour = 7/8 cup stone-ground whole wheat flour
2 cups granulated sugar = 1 pound
2¾ cups brown sugar = 1 pound

1 cup granulated sugar = 1 cup brown sugar or 1 cup raw sugar (not so sweet)
1 cup molasses = 13 ounces
5 large eggs = 1 cup
8 egg whites = 1 cup
16 egg yolks = 1 cup
2 cups butter = 1 pound
4 cups grated cheese = 1 pound
2 cups ground meat = 1 pound
1 cup uncooked rice = 2 cups cooked
1 cup uncooked macaroni = 2 cups cooked
1 cup uncooked noodles = 1¼ cups cooked
1 large lemon = ¼ cup juice
1 medium orange = ½ cup juice
2 cups dates = 1 pound
3 cups dried apricots = 1 pound
2½ cups prunes = 1 pound
2½ cups raisins = 1 pound
1½ pounds apples = 1 quart
3 large bananas = 1 pound
1 cup nut meats = 5 ounces
1 pound potatoes = 4 medium-sized potatoes
1 pound tomatoes = 3 medium-sized tomatoes
1 egg is equal in leavening power to ½ tsp baking powder

## Kitchen Math with Metric Tables

| MEASURE | EQUIVALENT | METRIC (ml) |
|---|---|---|
| 1 tablespoon | 3 teaspoons | 14.8 milliliters |
| 2 tablespoons | 1 ounce | 29.6 milliliters |
| ¼ cup | 4 tablespoons | 59.2 milliliters |
| ⅓ cup | 5 tablespoons, plus 1 teaspoon | 78.9 milliliters |
| ½ cup | 8 tablespoons | 118.4 milliliters |
| 1 cup | 16 tablespoons | 236.8 milliliters |
| 1 pint | 2 cups | 473.6 milliliters |
| 1 quart | 4 cups | 947.2 milliliters |
| 1 liter | 4 cups, plus 3⅓ tablespoons | 1,000.00 milliliters |
| 1 ounce (dry) | 2 tablespoons | 28.35 grams |
| 1 pound | 16 ounces | 453.59 grams |
| 2.21 pounds | 35.3 ounces | 1.00 kilogram |

# *Substitutions*

Remember that substitutions are just that. The original ingredient specified is always preferable.

| **If you don't have:** | **Substitute:** |
| --- | --- |
| 1 cup sour milk or buttermilk | 1 cup sweet milk mixed with one of the following: 1 tbsp vinegar, or 1 tbsp lemon juice, or 1¾ tsps cream of tartar, or 3 to 4 tbsps dried buttermilk, plus 1 cup water |
| 1 tbsp cornstarch | 2 tbsps flour or 2 tbsps quick-cooking tapioca |
| 1 cup brown sugar | 1 cup white sugar plus 1 tbsp molasses (stir into sugar) |
| 1 cup nuts | 1 cup coarse bran or Grapenuts, or 1 cup crushed corn flakes, plus ¼ tsp almond flavoring |
| 1 cup honey | 1¼ cups sugar plus ¼ cup liquid (whatever liquid is called for), or 1 cup molasses (flavor will be stronger) |
| 1 cup molasses | 1 cup honey (flavor will be mild) |
| 1 cup butter | 1 cup margarine, or 7/8 cup shortening plus ½ tsp salt, or 7/8 cup lard plus ½ tsp salt |
| 1 cup heavy cream | ⅓ cup butter, plus 7/8 cup milk |
| 1 cup whole milk | 1 cup reconstituted nonfat dry milk plus 2½ tsps butter or margarine, or ½ cup evaporated milk plus ½ cup water, or ¼ cup sifted dry whole milk plus 7/8 cup water |
| 1 tsp baking powder | ¼ tsp baking soda plus 5/8 tsp cream of tartar |
| 1 egg | 2 egg yolks; if you're short 1 egg in 3, use 2 eggs plus 1 tsp cornstarch |

## Miscellaneous Helpful Hints

• Now that my husband and I are alone at home, I slice the bread when it cools and slip it into a plastic bag, then freeze it and remove only the number of slices we need that day. Then we don't have stale bread sitting around, and we're not tempted to eat more bread than we should.

• If you have a bread failure (too light and crumbly, for example) or if bread becomes stale and a little dry, save it, don't waste it. Stale bread, two or three slices at a time, can be cut into tiny cubes, placed in plastic bags and frozen. You will have crumbs for casserole toppings or stuffing for turkey, or for apple brown betty, or for any recipe calling for bread crumbs.

• Croutons can be made from day-old (or older) bread. Butter the slices, cut into small cubes, and toast in a 350° F. oven for ten minutes. If desired, flavor with seasoning salts of your choice. Stack three or four slices together and cut them all at once. Store any leftover croutons in a tight-fitting container. If they become soggy at all, just crisp for three or four minutes in a 350° F. oven.

• Soggy crackers can be crisped by spreading them on a cookie sheet and baking at 350° F. 2 to 3 minutes.

• Whole-grain flours should be kept in a cool place if used within a week. Refrigerate if kept longer. All flours can be frozen.

• Wheat germ should always be refrigerated.

• The more yeast that is added to bread dough, the greater its nutritive value and the quicker the dough rises. Please use wisdom, however, and stick pretty much to the amounts in the recipes. Texture of bread or rolls is finer if the rising is not hurried. If possible, allow for two rising periods, at least. If you are not rushed, you can use less yeast for economy and allow approximately half again as much rising time.

• If you get a little too much milk in your biscuit dough, make spoon biscuits instead of rolled. Drop spoonfuls of dough onto a greased baking sheet. Bake at 425° F. to 450° F. twelve to fifteen minutes.

• Allow raisins to stand in hot water for a few minutes to plump them and keep them from sticking to the food chopper when ground.

• If a bit of egg yolk gets into the whites, the whites will not beat well. Moisten a cloth or paper towel with cold water and touch it to the yolk, which will adhere to the cloth.

• If dates are stuck together and dry, put them on a pie plate and warm them in a 200° F. oven a few minutes. They can then be separated easily.

• If cream has soured, it can be sweetened by adding a pinch of soda. Up to a teaspoon per pint can be added if necessary. If milk is beginning to turn sour, add a little soda, up to a tablespoon per quart, to make it last another day or two.

• Restore dry, unjuicy lemons by boiling them whole for five minutes. Soak lemons in warm water for several minutes before using, and they will give twice as much juice.

• Bread, frozen or thawed, can be reheated for unexpected guests by wrapping bread, as many slices as needed, in aluminum foil and placing it in a preheated 350° F. oven for twenty to thirty minutes. Guests will think it's freshly baked. Of course, a microwave oven is a miracle. In using a microwave oven, however, never reheat more bread than will be consumed immediately and limit the time to avoid toughness.

• When freezing bread, put in a strip of paper towel, which will usually prevent crystals from forming in the plastic bag.

## Kernels of Bread History

Perhaps some brief historical facts about bread will stimulate your appreciation of your role as bread baker for your family.

Bread is commonly known as the staff of life. Prehistoric man mixed milk or water with meal or flour to form dough, shaping it into cakes which were cooked on hot stones. The meal or flour was made from many seeds, herbs, or grains from grasses. The reason we generally eat bread made from wheat flour is that it contains a comparatively higher protein content than other grains and its greater gluten content gives elasticity.

Bread, as we know it today, is far removed from primitive efforts. The Egyptians learned how to make dough puff up. Spores from yeast plants fell into the dough, causing fermentation; they saved some of this paste for use in the next batch and "yeast" was born. The Egyptians also made the first oven, which was a round vessel of brick, the top narrowing to a cone shape. Orientals steamed their bread, later constructing a box with fire in the bottom and a partition which kept the bread above the fire. This was the forerunner of today's ovens fired with gas or electricity, thermostatically controlled and very easy to use.

In biblical times women ground their own grain between stones and made their own bread, both leavened and unleavened. Unleavened bread was used for the Passover, as it still is, to commemorate their flight into the wilderness from the persecutions of the Pharaoh when they took their unleavened dough with them and had to bake it afterward. (Exodus 12:39.)

The Romans made "milling machines" to grind grain into flour between two circular stones. One stone turned; the other was stationary. Romans developed bread making into an art. By 100 B.C. Rome sustained 285 bakeries. Bakers' guilds sprang up. Bakers were so highly esteemed that they became public officers.

In medieval England, lords of the manors built mills which they rented to millers; this forced anyone who had grain to grind to use the lord's mill and miller. The miller therefore became one of the most important persons in the community. Remember how the old fairy tales tell stories of the miller and the miller's daughter? They had ready audience with the king, or lord, because the millers held the key to the breadbaskets of the kingdom.

Then town bakeries were established. Householders took their flour to the baker to be baked into bread. In time the bakery, as we know it, evolved.

With so many unknown additives today, there is great security in being able to grind one's own flour at home and actually know what is being consumed. Bakers' and truckers' strikes need not be a serious concern if we have the stored necessities in our own homes and *the skill to use them.*

Throughout time, different cultures have regarded bread in different ways. In some cultures, "breaking bread" with a family makes you blood brothers. You enter into the soul of that home.

Natives of Morocco regard bread as holy food and they remove their shoes when eating bread.

In India, some religious sects stand when eating anything but bread, but they kneel to eat bread.

Sicilians deem it a sacrilege to eat bread with their hats on.

Millions of Hindus repeat from their prayer book: "Everything is food, but bread is the great mother."

Today, all too often bread is simply measured and evaluated by calories. Too many consumers fail to realize the nutritional value of bread. They pass it up in favor of calorie-laden sweets. Breads are part of the grain group, which is one of the necessary daily basic foods. The privilege of supplying our families with that "basic" should be appreciated and guarded.

*"What you try to do for others, you actually do for yourself."*
Anonymous

# Index